Talk Greek

Alison Kakoura
and
Karen Rich

Series editor
Alwena Lamping

Educational Publishers LLP trading as BBC Active
Edinburgh Gate
Harlow
Essex CM20 2JE
England

First published 1998
Revised and updated 2004
Reprinted 2004, 2005 (twice)
Second impression 2006

ISBN: 0563 520213

Project manager: Tamsen Harward
Edited by Virginia Masardo
Additional editing by Josie Frame, Mary Morton and Maria Dikeakou-Gaffney
Design management by Book Creation Services
Design by Avril Broadley for BCS
Illustrations by Sylvie Rabbe, Beatriz Waller and David Degreef-Mounier for BCS
Typeset by Gene Ferber for BCS
Production manager: Stephanie McConnell
Cover design by Helen Williams and Matt Bookman
Cover photographs: Matton Images UK
Audio producer: John Green, tefl tapes
Sound engineer: Tim Woolf
Presenters: Katya David; Zac Day; Maria Dikeakou-Gaffney; Tasos Spiridakis; Lucy Christy
Studio: Q Sound
Music by: Peter Hutchings

Printed and bound in Great Britain by Martins-the-Printers

The Publisher's policy is to use paper manufactured from sustainable forests.

Contents

Introduction   4
Pronunciation guide   6

1 Καλημέρα!   7
saying hello and goodbye
. . . and how are you?
saying what you're called
. . . and asking someone else's name

2 Από πού είσαστε;   15
saying what nationality you are
. . . and where you're from
saying if you're on holiday or business
using the numbers 0 to 12

3 Αυτός είναι ο Βαγγέλης   23
introducing friends and family
saying how old you are
talking about family

4 Ένα καφέ παρακαλώ   31
ordering a drink and a snack
offering someone a drink
accepting or refusing a drink

Έλεγχος! 1   39
progress check 1

5 Υπάρχει τράπεζα εδώ;   43
asking what facilities are available
. . . and how to find them
understanding basic directions
. . . and asking for help to understand

6 Πού μένετε;   51
talking about where you live and work
finding out where places are
. . . and when they are open

7 Πόσο κάνει;   59
asking for something in a shop
saying how much you want
asking the price of something
understanding amounts

Έλεγχος! 2   67
progress check 2

8 Θέλω ένα δωμάτιο   71
checking in at reception
finding a hotel room
booking ahead
making requests

9 Τι ώρα φεύγει;   79
asking about public transport
finding out travel times
buying tickets
checking travel details

10 Καλή όρεξη!   87
asking what's on the menu
ordering food and drink
expressing likes and dislikes
asking for more

Έλεγχος! 3   95
progress check 3

Reference section
Audio scripts and answers   99
Grammar   119
Greek-English glossary   123

Introduction

Welcome to **Talk Greek**, the BBC's new Greek course for absolute
beginners. Designed for adults, learning alone or in a class, it provides
the ideal introduction to Greek, covering the basic language needed
in everyday situations on a visit to Greece or Cyprus. It is suitable if
you want to learn for work, for fun and to prepare for a first-level
qualification.

Talk Greek is an interactive course consisting of a book and two
60-minute cassettes or CDs of recordings made by native Greek
speakers. Although designed to be used with the audio, the book
could be used separately as the audio scripts are included in the
reference section. Free tutors' support and activities are available
online at http://www.bbclanguages.com/talk/.

Talk Greek encourages you to make genuine progress and
promotes a real sense of achievement. The key to its effectiveness
lies in its structure and its systematic approach.
Key features include:

- simple step-by-step presentation of new language
- involvement and interaction at every stage
- regular progress checks
- useful hints on study skills and language learning
  strategies

How to use **Talk Greek**

Each of the ten units is completed in ten easy-to-follow steps.

I   Read the first page of the unit to focus on what you are
      aiming to learn and note any key vocabulary in the
      στην Ελλάδα και στην Κύπρο . . . (In Greece and in Cyprus . . .)
      section. This provides useful and relevant information on
      Greece and Cyprus and sets your learning in context.

2   Listen to the key phrases – don't be tempted to read them
      first. Then listen to them again, this time reading them in your
      book too. Finally, try reading them out loud before listening
      one more time. In the first four units new words and phrases
      have been transliterated (i.e. the sounds are written in English)
      to help you recognize the sounds as you read them, and to
      help your pronunciation as you read and speak them.

3   Work your way, step by step, through the activities that
      follow the key phrases. These highlight key language elements

and are carefully designed to develop your listening skills and your understanding of Greek. When you hear the activity number, pause the audio and read the instructions before you listen. To check your answers, refer to the *Audio scripts and answers* starting on page 99.

4 Read the *στα Ελληνικά . . . (in Greek . . .)* explanations of how the language works as you come to them – they are placed just where you need that information.

5 When you have completed the activities, and before you try the *Put it all together* section, close your book and listen to the Greek conversations straight through. The more times you listen, the more familiar the language will become and the more comfortable you will become with it. You might also like to read the dialogues at this stage.

6 Complete the consolidation activities on the *Put it all together* page and check your answers with the *Audio scripts and answers*. In the first four units, the activities on this page have been specifically designed to help you learn the alphabet. The alphabet strips are there as a constant reference for you to use with the pronunciation guide on page 6. Both these learning guides will help when you wish to start writing Greek.

7 Use the language you've learnt – the presenters on the audio will prompt you and guide you through the *Now you're talking!* page as you practise speaking Greek.

8 Check your progress. First, test your knowledge with the quiz. Then check whether you can do everything on the checklist – if in doubt, go back and spend some more time on the relevant section. You'll have further opportunities to test your knowledge in each *Έλεγχος! (Checkpoint)* after units 4, 7 and 10.

9 Read the learning hint at the end of the unit, which provides ideas and suggestions on how to use your study time effectively or how to extend your knowledge.

10 Finally, relax and listen to the whole unit, understanding what the people are saying in Greek and taking part in the conversations. This time you may not need the book so you can listen to the audio on its own.

Pronunciation guide

The best way to acquire a good Greek accent is to listen to the audio often and to imitate the speakers closely. In Greek, the spelling and pronunciation of letters is consistent, i.e. each letter and the letter combinations sound the same whenever they appear.

1 Here is the Greek alphabet with corresponding English sounds:

α	cat	ν	net
β	very	ξ	fax
γ*	ugly	ο	pot
γ§	yes	π	pepper
δ	mother	ρ	three
ε	hem	σ/ς	sweets
ζ	zip	τ	ten
η	meet	υ	meet
θ	think	φ	fun
ι	meet	χ*	Loch Ness
κ	king	χ§	huge
λ	lemon	ψ	copse
μ	map	ω	pot

* followed by ω, ο, α, ου, αυ and all consonants
§ followed by ε, η, ι, υ, αι, ει, οι and ευ

2 Certain letter combinations also produce specific sounds:

αι	hem	μπ	bed, or amber (if mid-word)
ει	meet	ντ	doctor, or under (if mid-word)
οι	meet	γκ	goal, or angle (if mid-word)
ου	soon	γγ	angle
αυ	have/raft	γχ	Birmingham
ευ	never/left		

3 Greek words with more than one syllable carry an accent ΄ to show which sound in the word is stressed. In spoken Greek, getting the stress right is as important as good pronunciation.

Καλημέρα!

- saying hello and goodbye

  . . . and how are you?

- saying what you are called

  . . . and asking someone else's name

στην Ελλάδα και στην Κύπρο . . .
(Pronounced steen Ellhadha keh steen Keepro)

(In Greece and in Cyprus . . .)

people tend to be informal with each other and
seldom use each other's surnames. You may well hear
people addressed as, for example, 'Mr George'
(**Κύριε Γιώργο**), or 'Mrs. Anna' (**Κυρία Άννα**),
which expresses both respect and friendliness.
As a visitor to these countries you will no doubt
experience the same informality.

Saying hello and goodbye . . .

I Listen to these key phrases.

Καλημέρα (σας)!　　　　　　　Good morning/day (to you)!
Kaleem**e**ra (sass)

Γεια σας! / Γεια σου!　　　　　Hello! (formal / informal)
Y**a**ssass / Y**a**ssoo　　　　　　　Goodbye!

(Note: the letters in bold in the transliterated words denote the stressed sounds in the Greek words.)

2 Listen as these people greet each other. Tick which greeting is used by each person as you hear it.

	I	2	3	4
Good morning	▬	▬	▬	▬
Hello	▬	▬	▬	▬

στα Ελληνικά . . . (in Greek . . .)

in general, **γειά σου** is used to address one person, and **γειά σας** is used for more than one person. However, to address one person more formally, e.g. a business contact, use **γειά σας**. The **σας** at the end of **Καλημέρα** makes this greeting more formal. The same rule applies to **Καλησπέρα (σας)**, Kaleespera (sass), (Good evening).

3 Listen to a group of Greek friends greeting each other. Look carefully at the names below and number each one as you hear it mentioned.

Μαρία ❑　　**Πάνο** ❑　　**Άννα** ❑　　**Στέλιο** ❑
(Mar**ee**a)　　(P**a**no)　　(**A**nna)　　(St**e**hlio)

Γειά σας and **Γειά σου** can also be used to mean 'goodbye'. Alternatively, you can say **αντίο** (and**ee**o), or, more formally, **αντίο σας** (goodbye to you).

. . . and how are you?

4 Listen to these key phrases.

Τι κάνετε; / Τι κάνεις; Tee kaneteh? / Tee kaneece?	How are you? (formal / informal)
(Πολύ) καλά! (Polee) kala	(Very) well!
Και εσείς; / Και εσύ; Keh eseece? / Keh esee?	And you? (formal / informal)
Έτσι κ'έτσι (Etsee k'etsee)	So-so

5 Listen to two short dialogues. How many times do you hear the question **Τι κάνετε;**?

στα Ελληνικά . . .

when talking to a person you are familiar with or wish to address less formally, e.g. a child, use the informal form, **τι κάνεις;** instead of **τι κάνετε;** and **εσύ** instead of **εσείς**.

Did you notice the Greek question mark? **;**

6 Listen to two more conversations on your audio. Can you distinguish between the formal and the informal?

7 Which of these Greek phrases would be appropriate when talking to:

		α	**Καλημέρα σας!**
1	two children	β	**Τι κάνεις;**
2	a business associate	γ	**Γεια σου!**
3	Stavros, a friendly waiter	δ	**Εσείς;**
		ε	**Τι κάνετε;**
		ζ	**Γεια σας!**
		η	**Εσύ;**
		θ	**Καλημέρα!**

Saying what you're called . . .

1 Listen to these key phrases.

Με λένε (Τομ)
Me leneh (Tom)

I'm called (Tom)

Πώς σας λένε;
Poss sass leneh?

What are you called? (formal)

Πώς σε λένε;
Poss se leneh?

What are you called? (informal)

2 Some of the participants at a trade fair in Athens have been given incorrect name tags. Listen to three people giving their names and match their first names with their surnames.

Αλέκος

Σαμαράκης

Παππά

Κατερίνα

Μάνος

Καπετάνιος

στα Ελληνικά . . .

many male names and surnames end in '**ς**'. However, this letter is omitted when:

– saying what you are called: **Νίκος Σερετάκης** would say:
  Με λένε Νίκο Σερετάκη.
– addressing or greeting someone by name:
  Γεια σου, Νίκο! or **Καλημέρα σας, Κύριε Σερετάκη!**

---

3 Listen to these four young people greeting each other:

Γιάννης   **Ιωάννα**   **Αλίκη**   **Σπύρος**
(Yannis)   (Yoanna)   (Aleeki)   (Speeros)

How would each of them respond to the question **Πώς σε λένε;**?

4 How would *you* respond to the above question?

. . . and asking someone else's name

5 Listen to Costas, a tourist guide in Thessaloniki, checking the names of people on an excursion.

Notice how he uses the informal question **Πώς σε λένε;** when addressing the younger members of the party.

Complete the dialogue below by filling the gaps with the appropriate numbers from the box on the right.

Κώστας	**Καλημέρα! Πώς σας _____;**
Νίκος	**_____ λένε Νίκο Σερετάκη.**
Κώστας	**Πώς _____ λένε;**
Μαρία	**Μαρία Παππά.**
Κώστας	**Γειά _____! Πώς σε λένε;**
Αλίκη	**Με λένε Αλίκη. Αλίκη Σαμαρά.**
Κώστας	**_____ σε λένε;**
Σπύρος	**Σπύρο Σαμαρά.**

σας (1)
Με (2)
λένε (3)
Πώς (4)
σου (5)

6 Listen to some more people being asked their names. Circle the appropriate word below to indicate which people are addressed formally and which informally.

α **Νίκος**   formal / informal
β **Άννα**   formal / informal
γ **Γιάννης**   formal / informal
δ **Μαρία**   formal / informal

Put it all together

Here's the Greek alphabet.

A B Γ Δ Ε Ζ Η Θ Ι Κ Λ Μ Ν Ξ Ο Π Ρ Σ Τ Υ Φ Χ Ψ Ω
α β γ δ ε ζ η θ ι κ λ μ ν ξ ο π ρ σ/ς τ υ φ χ ψ ω

I Can you find six Greek letters from the words on pages 8 to 11 that sound like English letters and look like them in both capitals and lower case?

2 Link the capitals with the lower case letters in the box below by drawing a line between them — then check with the alphabet above.

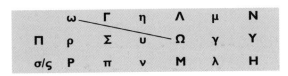

Notice the two lower case versions of the Greek letter **Σ**: (σ and ς). ς is only used at the end of a word.

3 Write the number of the Greek letter that matches the equivalent English sound shown in bold print in the words below. (If you need help, refer to the phonetic version of the key phrases).

I	γ	☐	**m**an
2	η and υ	☐	**p**ull
3	λ	☐	**s**un
4	μ	☐	**t**ee
5	ν	☐	**h**o**t**
6	π	☐	**l**id
7	ρ	☐	**y**es
8	σ / ς	☐	**r**ed
9	ω and ο	☐	**n**et

4 Read the key phrases again while listening to them on your audio. Notice the accent ◆ indicating which sound in a word is stressed.

Now you're talking!

I   Imagine you're Stelios Kappas, a Greek businessman staying at a hotel owned by your friends Panos and Katerina. You introduce yourself to a visitor at the bar before your friends arrive with their daughter Aliki. Prepare your part in the dialogues then be guided by the presenter on the audio.

- ◆ Say good evening.
- ◇ **Καλησπέρα σας!**
- ◆ Tell him your name and ask him his.
- ◇ **Με λένε Αντώνη Κορέλλη.**

Panos and Katerina join you.
- ◆ Greet each of them by name and say 'hello!'
- ◇ **Γεια σου, Στέλιο! Τι κάνεις;**
- ◆ Say: 'Very well, and you?'
- ◇ **Καλά, καλά!**

Now Aliki comes in.
- ◆ Greet her and ask her how she is.
- ◇ **Έτσι κ'έτσι!**

2   How would you respond to these greetings and questions?

- ◇ **Καλημέρα σας!**
- ◇ **Πώς σας λένε;**
- ◇ **Τι κάνετε;**
- ◆ (add, 'and you?')
- ◆ (and as you leave) **Αντίο!**

Quiz

1 Which phrase can mean both 'hello' and 'goodbye'?
2 What can you add to **Καλημέρα** to make it more formal?
3 How would you greet your friend Costas by name?
4 How would you say 'hello' to more than one person?
5 If you wanted to ask a new business associate how they were, would you say **Τι κάνεις;** or **Τι κάνετε;**?
6 What does the sign ; indicate in Greek?
7 How would you ask a child his or her name?
8 What does the expression **έτσι κ'έτσι** mean?
9 Which of these letters both look and sound the same in English?
 M E I P H A K N T O
10 What are the nearest equivalent English sounds to the following Greek letters? **σ π λ η ω γ ν**

Now check whether you can . . .

- ■ say 'good morning'

- ■ say 'hello' and 'goodbye'

- ■ ask someone how they are

- ■ reply when someone asks how you are

- ■ say 'and you?' – formally and informally

- ■ ask someone's name and say what you are called

- ■ recognize and use formal and informal forms of the above

You can use the alphabet strip at the top of pages 12, 20, 28 and 36 in several ways. For example it can be used for reference, and when you are able to pronounce the individual sounds that the letters represent, you can use it as a checklist. You can also enlarge the script and use it to practise writing the letters. Saying the sounds out loud as you write them will reinforce your recognition of both lower case and capital letters. It will also help your pronunciation.

Από πού είσαστε;

- saying what nationality you are
  ... and where you're from
- saying if you're on holiday or business
- using the numbers 0 to 12

στην Ελλάδα και στην Κύπρο . . .

you are sure to find yourself in conversation with friendly people who will be very curious to know about you, who you are and where you're from, especially if you speak a little Greek. They in turn will be delighted to tell you about themselves. So you'll find it useful to know how to talk about yourself – and to ask others a few questions too.

Saying what nationality you are . . .

| Listen to these key phrases.

Είσαστε Άγγλος / Αγγλίδα;
Eesasteh Anglos / Angleedha?)

Are you English? (m. / f.)

Ναι / Όχι
Neh / Ohee

Yes / No

Είμαι Σκωτσέζος / Σκωτσέζα
Eemeh Scotsehzos / Scotsehza

I'm Scottish (m. / f.)

στα Ελληνικά . . .

the words describing nationality have different endings for masculine
and feminine. An English man would say **είμαι Άγγλος**, whereas an
English woman would say **είμαι Αγγλίδα**. Here are some more
examples:

	Greek	American	Irish
male	**Έλληνας**	**Αμερικανός**	**Ιρλανδός**
female	**Ελληνίδα**	**Αμερικανίδα**	**Ιρλανδέζα**

For a more informal way of saying 'you are' and 'are you?' replace
είσαστε with **είσαι** (eeseh) e.g. **είσαι Έλληνας;**

---

2   Listen as Eleni, a language tutor in a Greek summer school, finds out
    about her new students. Match the names and nationalities by ticking
    the box.

	English	Scottish	Irish	American
John	▦	▦	▦	▦
Linda	▦	▦	▦	▦
Peter	▦	▦	▦	▦
Ann	▦	▦	▦	▦

3   Now listen to Eleni talking to Patsy and Paul, two younger members of
    the group. What nationality are they?

. . . and where you're from

4 Listen to these key phrases.

Από πού είσαστε / είσαι;
Apo poo eesasteh / eeseh?

Where are you from? (formal / informal)

Είμαι από την Αγγλία
Eemeh apo teen Angleea

I'm from England

Δεν είμαι από την Ελλάδα
Dhen eemeh apo teen Elladha

I'm not from Greece

5 A tourist guide in Cyprus is asking four people where they're from. Number the countries in the order you hear them. Then match the English names with the Greek.

.... America   **Αγγλία**
.... Greece   **Σκωτία**
.... England   **Αμερική**
.... Scotland   **Ελλάδα**

στα Ελληνικά . . .

the word **δεν** placed before words like **είμαι** and **είσαστε** makes a statement or a question negative:

(Δεν) είμαι από την Αγγλία   I'm (not) from England
(Δεν) είσαστε από την Αγγλία;   Are (n't) you from England?

6 Now listen as Eleni gets to know Haris, a new tutor. Note the informal form of the question:
Εσύ Ελένη, από πού είσαι;

Where is Eleni from?
What part of Greece is Haris from?

Saying if you're on holiday or business

1 Listen to these key phrases.

Είσαστε εδώ για δουλειά;   Are you here for work?
Eesasteh edh**o** yeea dhool**ee**a?

(Δεν) είμαι εδώ για διακοπές I'm (not) here on holiday
(Dhen) **ee**meh edh**o** yeea dheeakop**es**

2 Listen to two people talking in their hotel. Are they both on holiday?

3 In the next dialogue two people meet for the first time. Listen and fill
   in the information about them in the box below.

	Man	Woman
Name	....	....
Nationality	....	....
From . . .	....	....
On holiday?	....	....

Using the numbers 0 to 12

I Listen to the numbers 1 to 12 paying particular attention to where the stress falls in each word. Repeat them aloud, putting special emphasis on the stressed sounds.

1 **ένα**	(e**nn**a)	7 **εφτά**	(eft**a**)
2 **δύο**	(dh**ee**o)	8 **οχτώ**	(ocht**o**)
3 **τρία**	(tr**ee**a)	9 **εννιά**	(enni**a**)
4 **τέσσερα**	(t**e**ssera)	10 **δέκα**	(dh**e**ka)
5 **πέντε**	(p**e**ndeh)	11 **ένδεκα**	(**e**ndheka)
6 **έξι**	(**e**xee)	12 **δώδεκα**	(dh**o**dheka)

2 Listen to Eleni telling her language students their room numbers as she hands out the keys. Circle the numbers below as you hear them.

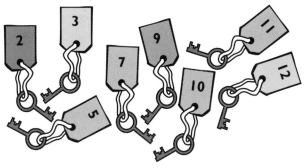

3 In your room you tune your radio to a Greek station and hear the results of some English football matches. Listen and fill in the scores. Note the word **μηδέν** (meedh**e**n) meaning 'nil' or 'zero'.

Liverpool	☐	☐	Arsenal
Blackburn	☐	☐	Manchester United
Newcastle	☐	☐	Everton
Leeds	☐	☐	Chelsea
Wimbledon	☐	☐	Southampton

Put it all together

Focus on the highlighted sounds.

| A B Γ **Δ** E **Z** H **Θ** I K Λ M N **Ξ** O Π P Σ T Y **Φ X Ψ** Ω |
| α **β** γ **δ** ε **ζ** η **θ** ι κ λ μ ν **ξ** ο π ρ σ/ς τ υ **φ χ ψ** ω |

I   Can you work out how to pronounce these Greek names, which all contain letters and sounds you have met in this unit? Check your pronunciation with the audio.

Δράμα Λάζαρος Αντίπαξος Χάρης Πάφος Χίος Πάργα

For pronunciation of the letters **γ** and **χ** see page 6.

2   Now listen to the following words. Then repeat them, paying particular attention to three new sounds: **Bβ   Θθ   Ψψ**

ταβέρνα	**θέατρο**	**διψομανία**
(tav**eh**rna)	(t**h**e**h**atro)	(dheepsoman**ee**a)

What do you think these words mean?

3   Write the name of each country in the empty column. Then link each one to the corresponding nationality by drawing a line between the two. One has been done for you.

COUNTRY   NATIONALITY

masculine   feminine

		masculine	feminine
Greece	**ΕΛΛΑΔΑ**	Άγγλος	Αγγλίδα
....	**ΚΥΠΡΟΣ**	Ουαλός	Ουαλή
....	**ΑΓΓΛΙΑ**	Έλληνας	Ελληνίδα
....	**ΣΚΩΤΙΑ**	Κύπριος	Κύπρια
....	**ΟΥΑΛΙΑ**	Αυστραλός	Αυστραλέζα
....	**ΙΡΛΑΝΔΙΑ**	Σκωτσέζος	Σκωτσέζα
....	**ΑΥΣΤΡΑΛΙΑ**	Αμερικανός	Αμερικανίδα
....	**ΑΜΕΡΙΚΗ**	Ιρλανδός	Ιρλανδέζα

" Now you're talking!

I You're on a ferry and you'd like to practise your Greek by talking to
the woman sitting next to you. Work out how you would:

◆ greet her and ask if she's Greek (**Είσαστε Ελληνίδα;**)
◆ ask where she's from
◆ say where you're from
◆ say what you're called

● Where is she from?

2 Imagine you're Sam Collins, an American from Atlanta on business in
Cyprus, answering questions for a survey. Work out how you would
reply to these questions before listening to the audio.

◇ **Πώς σας λένε;**
◆ You
◇ **Είσαστε Άγγλος;**
◆ You
◇ **Από πού είσαστε;**
◆ You
◇ **Είσαστε εδώ για δουλειά;**

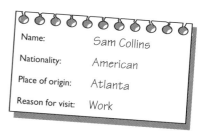

Name: Sam Collins
Nationality: American
Place of origin: Atlanta
Reason for visit: Work

3 While eating at a taverna, you are recognised and greeted by the local
baker who is also eating there with his family. Note the informal tone.

◇ **Καλημέρα!**
◆ You
◇ **Τι κάνεις;**
◆ You
◇ **Από πού είσαι;**
◆ You
◇ **Είσαι εδώ για διακοπές;**
◆ You

Quiz

1 How do you tell someone you're from Scotland?
2 Would a Greek man say **είμαι Ελληνίδα** or **είμαι Έλληνας**?
3 Can you put the numbers below into the correct order?
   εφτά   δύο   δώδεκα   μηδέν   πέντε   εννιά
4 Which numbers between 0 and 12 are missing in question 3?
   Practise saying them.
5 How do you say: 'I'm here on holiday.'?
6 Which of these Greek words is the odd one out? Why?
   Αγγλία   Ιρλανδέζα   Ελληνίδα
7 How do you make this Greek sentence mean: 'I'm not from Wales.'?
   Είμαι από την Ουαλία
8 How do you make the statement **Είσαστε καλά** into a question
   meaning: 'Are you well?' (in written and spoken forms)?
9 How do you ask a child where s/he is from?
10 Can you identify these English names which have been written in
   Greek letters? **Μαξ   Πήτερ   Βήρα   Λόρενς   Κάθριν**

Now check whether you can . . .

- ◼ say what nationality you are and where you're from

- ◼ say if you're on holiday or on business

- ◼ ask others for this information

- ◼ identify questions and negatives in written and spoken Greek

- ◼ say and recognize the numbers 0 to 12

Play your audio recording as much as possible to tune in to the
sounds and rhythm of Greek. From the start, listen often to reinforce
words and phrases you learn. Also, you can play the dialogues from
later units of the course before you actually study them just to pick
out sounds and words you might recognize — as you would when
'eavesdropping' on conversations in Greece or Cyprus.

3 τρία

Αυτός είναι
ο Βαγγέλης

- introducing friends
  . . . and family
- saying how old you are
- talking about family

στην Ελλάδα και στην Κύπρο . . .

when people are introduced to each other, it
is usual for them to shake hands. When they know
each other better, a kiss on both cheeks often
accompanies a greeting.

When meeting someone, even for the first time, it is
not considered impolite to ask questions such as
'How old are you?', or even, 'How much do you
earn?', so don't be offended if you are asked to reveal
such personal information!

Introducing friends . . .

1 Listen to these key phrases.

Αυτός είναι ο . . .
Aftos eeneh o . . .

This is . . . (to introduce a man)

Αυτός είναι ο Βαγγέλης
Aftos eeneh o Vangelis

This is Vangelis

Αυτή είναι η . . .
Aftee eeneh ee . . .

This is . . . (to introduce a woman)

Αυτή είναι η Ευγενία
Aftee eeneh ee Evyeneea

This is Eugenia

Χαίρω πολύ
Hairo polee

Pleased to meet you

στα Ελληνικά . . .

when introducing people by name you say, e.g. 'This is **the** Stella', 'this is **the** Stavros'. 'The' is **η** before female names and **o** before male names.

2 Listen as Eleni introduces two of her students to her friend Stella. Choose the correct word from the box to complete the dialogue.

Pam/Mike **Καλησπέρα, Ελένη!**

Eleni **Καλησπέρα σας! Στέλλα, ___ είναι ___ Μάικ και ___ είναι ___ Παμ.**

η	1
αυτός	2
αυτή	3
o	4

3 Eleni now introduces Stella to Mike and Pam. How do you think she will do it? Check with your audio.

. . . and family

4 Listen to these key phrases.

Αυτός είναι ο άντρας μου   This is my husband
Aftos eeneh o andras moo

Αυτή είναι η γυναίκα μου   This is my wife
Aftee eeneh ee yeenekka moo

Πώς τον / τη λένε;   What's he / she called?
Poss ton / tee leneh?

Τον / Τη λένε . . .   He / She's called . . .
Ton / tee leneh . . .

> **στα Ελληνικά . . .**
>
> 'my —' is expressed as 'the — of me', i.e. with either **o** or **η** before the word and **μου** after the word.
> 'Your' is expressed in the same way, with **σας** (formal) or **σου** (informal) after the word.

5 Listen and link the married couples.

Σούλα   **Όλγα**   **Χρήστος**   **Δημήτρης**

6 Listen as Stella points out her husband to Pam and circle the correct word from the alternatives below.

Stella   **Αυτός είναι ο άντρας μου.**
Pam   **Πώς τον / τη λένε;**
Stella   **Τον / Τη λένε Γιώργο.**

Saying how old you are

I   Listen to the following numbers 13 to 100.

13	δεκατρία	30	τριάντα
14	δεκατέσσερα	33	τριάντα τρία (etc.)
15	δεκαπέντε	40	σαράντα
16	δεκαέξι	44	σαράντα τέσσερα (etc.)
17	δεκαεφτά	50	πενήντα
18	δεκαοχτώ	60	εξήντα
19	δεκαεννιά	70	εβδομήντα
20	είκοσι	80	ογδόντα
21	είκοσι ένα	90	ενενήντα
22	είκοσι δύο (etc.)	100	εκατό(ν)

Note that **ντ** as in the numbers 30 to 90, is pronounced 'nd' in the middle of a word. (See the pronunciation guide on page 6.)

2   Listen to these numbers on your audio, then cross them out as you hear them spoken. Circle the numbers which are not mentioned.

92   76   13   29   31   64   85   21

3   Listen to these key phrases.

Πόσο χρονών είσαστε / είσαι;
Posso chronon eesasteh / eeseh?

How old are you? (formal / informal)

Είμαι 11 (χρονών)
Eemeh 11 (chronon)

I'm 11 (years old)

4   Now Mike asks Koula how old she is. Tick the correct age when you hear it.

69	61	29	21

26   **Αυτός είναι ο Βαγγέλης**

Talking about family

1 Listen to these key phrases.

Έχετε / Έχεις παιδιά;
Eheteh / Eheece pedheea?

Do you have any children? (formal / informal)

Έχω ένα παιδί
Eho enna pedhee

I have a/one child

Πόσο χρονών είναι;
Posso hronon eeneh?

How old is he/is she/are they?

2 Listen as Pam asks some of Eleni's colleagues about their families. Indicate below how many children each person has.

Τάκης ▨   **Άννα** ▨   **Κούλα** ▨

3 Listen again and circle the correct ages for Takis' children.

Ο Πέτρος είναι 19 / 17 χρονών;   Η Έλλη είναι 1 / 9 χρονών;
Η Μαρίνα είναι 11 / 12 χρονών;   Ο Γιάννης είναι 7 / 4 χρονών;

στα Ελληνικά . . .

to change 'I have' to 'you have' change the ending of the word **έχω** to **έχετε** or **έχεις**. Note also the changes to **είμαι**:

Είμαι   I am
Είσαι/Είσαστε   you are
Είναι   he/she/it is/they are

---

4 To complete these conversation exchanges, choose the appropriate words from the box below and number the gaps.

a **Γιάννη,** ....**παιδιά;**
   Ναι, ...**δύο.**
β **Παιδιά, πόσο χρονών**.................;
   ....**δέκα και ο Σάκης**
   ....**πέντε.**

| 1 Είμαι |
| 2 έχεις |
| 3 είσαστε |
| 4 έχω |
| 5 είναι |

Put it all together

A B Γ Δ E Z H Θ I K Λ M N Ξ O Π P Σ T Y Φ X Ψ Ω
α β γ δ ε ζ η θ ι κ λ μ ν ξ ο π ρ σ/ς τ υ φ χ ψ ω

I Look at the pronunciation guide and check with the audio how to pronounce the following letter combinations:

αι   ει   οι   ου   ευ   αυ   γγ

Listen to these words from the key phrases and repeat them to practise the above sounds:

γυν<u>αί</u>κα   <u>εί</u>ναι   μ<u>ου</u>   Ε<u>υ</u>γενία   <u>αυ</u>τός   Βα<u>γγ</u>έλης

2 The letter combination **οι** is pronounced 'ee'. How do you think the Greek word for 'family' **οικογένεια** is pronounced? Check your pronunciation with the audio.

3 Here are the names of some towns and cities in Britain and other places, written in Greek letters. See if you can recognize them – saying the names out loud should help.

Κρου   Ρέξαμ   Περθ   Λίμερικ   Βανκούβερ   Λέστερ Ουέλλιγγτον   Κιλμάρνοκ   Έψομ   Φοίνιξ

4 Can you rearrange the words in the sentences below, to mean:

α This is my wife Maria.
γυναίκα / Αυτή / η / μου / Μαρία / είναι / η

β I have one child, he's called Manoli.
παιδί, / Μανώλη / τον / Έχω / λένε / ένα

γ How old is your husband, Dora?
σου, / χρονών / Δώρα / Πόσο / άντρας / ο / είναι / ;

Now you're talking!

1   Imagine you're Debbie on holiday in Greece with your husband Simon. You fall into conversation with a Greek man while waiting for a ferry to one of the islands.

◆ Say 'Good morning'.
◇ **Καλημέρα σας!**
◆ Say 'Are you here on holiday?'
◇ **Ναι.**
◆ Ask him his name.
◇ **Με λένε Θωμά.**
◆ Say 'Is this your wife?'
◇ **Ναι. Είναι η Αφροδίτη.**
◆ Say 'Pleased to meet you'.
◆ Ask if he has any children.
◇ **Ναι. Δύο.**
◆ Ask how old they are.
◇ **Είναι 12 και 16 χρονών.**
◆ Introduce your husband.
◇ **Χαίρω πολύ!**

2   Now you're telling a Greek person about yourself. You need to know how to:

◆ say if you're on holiday or not
◆ say where you're from/what nationality you are
◆ say what you're called
◆ say how old you are
◆ say whether you have children or not, and how many

3   Practise introducing members of your own family and your friends and saying their names and ages. The following may be useful:

ο φίλος μου (o **fee**los moo)   my friend (male)
η φίλη μου (ee **fee**lee moo)   my friend (female)

Quiz

1 Would you use **αυτός είναι** or **αυτή είναι** to introduce a man?
2 If someone says: **Είμαι εξήντα εννιά χρονών** are they 21, 60 or 69?
3 **Αυτοί είναι οι φίλοι μου** means 'These are my friends'. How do you think this sentence should be pronounced?
4 When asking about a woman's name, should you say: **Πώς τη λένε;** or **Πώς τον λένε;**?
5 What is missing from the phrase: **Αυτός είναι Σταύρος**?
6 How would you say: 'My husband'?
7 'He/She is' in Greek is: **είμαι**, **είναι** or **είσαι**?
8 What is the Greek for: 20, 40, 70 and 100?
9 How would you say: 'I have three children.'?

Now check whether you can . . .

- ■ introduce someone, male or female

- ■ say whether you have children or not and how many

- ■ say your age

- ■ ask others for the same information

- ■ use the numbers 13 to 100

- ■ ask and say how old someone else is

Using photographs of your family and friends, you could practise introducing them, and giving details such as names and ages, to an imaginary listener. You could also practise being the listener and asking the relevant questions.

If you are talking about children, the words **αγόρια** (boys) and **κορίτσια** (girls) are useful. 'One boy' is **ένα αγόρι** and 'one girl' **ένα κορίτσι**. So you could practise asking and answering the question: **Τι είναι, αγόρια ή κορίτσια;** which means: 'What are they, boys or girls?'

4 τέσσερα

Ένα καφέ παρακαλώ

- ordering a drink
  - ... and a snack
- offering someone a drink
- accepting or refusing a drink

στην Ελλάδα και στην Κύπρο . . .

there are two types of café-bar. The **καφενείο** has traditionally been the domain of men drinking Greek coffee (**ελληνικός καφές**), which can be ordered either sweet (**γλυκό**), medium-sweet (**μέτριο**), or without sugar (**σκέτο**).

The **καφετερία** is still a meeting place for families and groups of friends. Many now offer continental-style coffee, as well as a wider range of alcoholic and non-alcoholic drinks and snacks. Alcoholic drinks such as **ούζο** (a typically Greek aniseed-flavoured aperitif) are normally taken with at least a snack, as Greeks and Cypriots rarely drink on an empty stomach.

Ordering a drink . . .

I   Listen to these key phrases.

Ένα καφέ παρακαλώ . . .   a / one coffee please . . .
Enna kaffeh parakalo

. . . και ένα τσάι   . . . and a / one tea
keh enna tsaee

Μία μπύρα παρακαλώ   a/one beer please
Meea beera parakalo

Ευχαριστώ (πολύ)   Thank you (very much)
Efharisto [polee]

Παρακαλώ   You're welcome
Parakalo

2   Listen to some friends ordering drinks in a **καφετερία**. Can you indicate with an arrow who drinks what?

| man I |
| man 2 |
| woman I |
| woman 2 |

λεμονάδα   μπύρα   τσάι   καφέ

στα Ελληνικά . . .

when ordering things, the word for 'a / one' can be either **ένα** or **μία**. Here, words ending in **-α** use **μία**, all the rest use **ένα**.

3   Listen as George orders drinks for his friends. Tick the drinks for which he uses **ένα** and put a cross by those for which he uses **μία**:

. . . and a snack

4 Listen to these key phrases.

Τι (καφέ) θέλετε;
Tee kaffeh theleteh
What (coffee) do you want?

Θέλω ένα ελληνικό καφέ
Thelo enna ellineeko kaffeh
I want a Greek coffee

Ένα Νεσκαφέ με γάλα
Enna neskaffeh meh ghala
an instant coffee with milk

Ένα τοστ με τυρί / ζαμπόν
Enna tost meh teeree / zambon
a toasted sandwich with cheese / ham

5 Listen to Amalia ordering a drink and a snack. What does she order?

6 Listen to the friends in the **καφετερία** ordering some snacks. Can you say who has what? You will hear the word **εντάξει** (endaxee), which means 'OK'.

| man 1 |
| man 2 |
| woman 1 |
| woman 2 |

τοστ παγωτό πάστα ομελέτα

7 Now how would you order the following?

a   Tea with milk and a cake.
β   A beer and a toasted sandwich with cheese.
γ   A ham omelette and a lemonade.
δ   An ice cream and a Greek coffee.

Offering someone a drink

I Listen to these key phrases.

Τι θα πάρετε / πάρεις;
Tee tha parehteh / pareece?

What will you have? (lit. 'what will you take?') (formal / informal)

Θα πάρω ένα ούζο
Tha paro enna ouzo

I'll have an ouzo . . .

. . . με νερό
. . . meh nehro

. . . with water

. . . χωρίς πάγο
. . . horeece pagho

. . . without ice

Ορίστε
Oreesteh

Here (you are)

2 Listen as Marcos offers his friend a drink. What would she like?

3 Eleni offers some of her students a drink in the bar. Can you tell who orders the following drinks? Listen out for **για μένα**, which means 'for me'.

α a gin and tonic ....

β an ouzo with water ....

γ a soda water with ice ....

4 How would you say you'll have:

α an instant coffee with milk?

β whisky without ice?

γ an ice cream?

Accepting or refusing a drink

I   Listen to these key phrases.

Θα πάρετε / πάρεις ένα ποτό;   Will you have a drink?
Tha parehteh / pareece enna poto?   (formal / informal)

Ναι / Όχι ευχαριστώ!   Yes / No thanks!
Neh / Ohee efharisto!

Στην υγειά σας / σου!   Cheers! / To your health!
Steen eeya sass / soo!   (formal / informal)

2   Listen to some people being offered the drinks illustrated below and indicate with a tick or a cross which are accepted and which are refused.

3   Listen to the dialogue on your audio. Note how when ordering Greek coffee (**ελληνικός καφές**), the final **ς** is omitted from each word.

a   What do you conclude about the kind of drink **ποτό** normally refers to?

β   Why do you think there are two different versions of the phrase 'To your health' in this conversation?

Put it all together

| Α Β Γ Δ Ε Ζ Η Θ Ι Κ Λ Μ Ν Ξ Ο Π Ρ Σ Τ Υ Φ Χ Ψ Ω |
| α β γ δ ε ζ η θ ι κ λ μ ν ξ ο π ρ σ/ς τ υ φ χ ψ ω |

I Here are some more letter combinations and the sounds they represent: **μπ** = 'b', **ντ** = 'd', **γκ** = 'g', **αϊ** = 'eye'. These are commonly used to represent sounds in borrowed or foreign words.

See if you can work out how to pronounce these words:
μπακλαβάς   ντισκοτέκ   γκαράζ   κανταΐφι

Can you say what they mean?

2 Can you write the missing letters in the following Greek words?

  κα__έ   **ο__ελέτα**   **ρετσί__α**   **ού__ο**
  (coffee)   (omelette)   (retsina)   (ouzo)
  παρακα__ώ   **σό__α**   **μπύ__α**
  (please)   (soda water)   (beer)

3 You see the following signs around the town. What do you think they say?

ΜΠΟΥΤΙΚ	**ΦΑΣΤ ΦΟΥΝΤ**	**ΚΑΜΠΙΝΓΚ**
	ΝΤΙΣΚΟΤΕΚ	**ΣΝΑΚΜΠΑΡ**
ΜΠΡΕΚΦΑΣΤ	**ΤΑΒΕΡΝΑ**	**ΤΑΞΙ**

4 Complete the following dialogue with words from the box below.

- **Καλησπέρα** .... **. Τι** .... **πάρετε;**
- .... **μπύρα για μένα, παρακαλώ.**
- **Εντάξει. Και εσείς;**
- .... **ούζο με πάγο.**
- **Και** .... **, κύριε;**
- **Θα** .... **ένα ελληνικό**
  .... **ένα κανταΐφι.**

Μία
και
πάρω
θα
σας
καφέ
Ένα
εσείς

Now you're talking!

I   You have invited your Greek business colleagues, Savvas and Arta, to the hotel bar for a drink. You ask what they would like and then you make your order. Use the informal form.

- ◆ Ask them if they will have a drink.
- ◊ **Ναι, ευχαριστώ! Ένα τζιν με τόνικ, παρακαλώ.**
- ◆ Ask Arta what she will have.
- ◊ **Μία μπύρα για μένα παρακαλώ.**
- ◆ Say OK. At the bar order their drinks, and a whisky for yourself.
- ◊ **Με πάγο;**
- ◆ Say 'no thanks'. As you give your guests their drinks say: 'Here you are'. . .
- ◊ **Ευχαριστούμε!** . . . and,
- ◆ 'To your health!'
- ◊ **Στην υγειά μας!**

Ευχαριστούμε means '**We** thank you' and **Στην υγειά μας** means 'To **our** health'.

2   You are in a **καφετερία** with a friend. Order a tea with milk and a Greek coffee. When asked, order two toasted sandwiches – one with ham and the other with cheese. When the waiter serves you, say thank you for both of you.

3   You are offered a drink in a **μπαρ** (bar) by your friend Costas. Accept the offer and say you'll have a vodka and lemonade. You prefer it without ice. Thank him and drink to his health.

4   Imagine yourself in a **καφετερία** with a group of close friends or family. Practise ordering drinks and/or snacks which you know these people would normally have.

Quiz

1 If you wanted lemon with your tea, would you order it:
   χωρίς λεμόνι or **με λεμόνι**?
2 Would you use **ένα** or **μία** to order the following items?
   καφέ   παγωτό   μπύρα   πάστα   τοστ   ούζο   ομελέτα
3 What are the two meanings of **παρακαλώ**?
4 If you wanted to drink to someone else's health, would you say:
   στην υγειά σας or **στην υγειά μας**?
5 How would you pronounce the name of this Athenian football team?
   Παναθηναϊκός
6 How do you say 'OK' in Greek?
7 What is **μπακλαβάς**?
8 Which combinations of Greek letters represent these sounds:
   'd'   'g'   'b'   'eye'?
9 How would you say: 'We thank you'?
10 How would you change **έχετε** (you have) to mean 'I have'?

Now check whether you can . . .

■ order a drink and/or a snack in a café or bar

■ offer someone a drink or snack

■ politely accept or refuse something

■ say whether you want your drink or snack with or without something

■ say 'to our/your health!'

Teaching another person the Greek words for various items could help you to remember them better yourself. So why not enlist the co-operation of a willing friend or member of the family, and when you are out with them, in a pub or a café, discuss how you would place your order for drinks and/or snacks in Greek?

Έλεγχος! 1

1 Costas is in conversation with one of his tour group who is being asked questions about herself. Listen and tick the correct boxes.

α	**Με λένε**	☐	**Σοφία**	☐	**Σόνια**
β	**Είμαι**	☐	**Αγγλίδα**	☐	**Ελληνίδα**
γ	**Ο άντρας μου είναι**	☐	**Αυστραλός**	☐	**Άγγλος**
δ	**Είμαι από την**	☐	**Αθήνα**	☐	**Αγγλία**
ε	**Έχω ένα**	☐	**κορίτσι**	☐	**αγόρι**
ζ	**Είναι**	☐	**20**	☐	**6**

2 Choose the right expression for the situations below.

α Accepting a drink
β Saying: 'Please'
γ Saying: 'Hello'
δ In reply to **Τι κάνετε;**
ε Saying: 'Pleased to meet you'
ζ Saying: 'Cheers!'
η Saying: 'And you?'
θ Saying something is all right

3 Match the phrases in column 1 with their appropriate responses.

1	**Τι κάνετε;**	*α*	**Μάρθα.**
2	**Είσαστε εδώ για διακοπές;**	*β*	**Καλά, ευχαριστώ.**
3	**Αυτή είναι η φίλη σας;**	*γ*	**Όχι, δεν είμαι.**
4	**Πώς τη λένε;**	*δ*	**Ναι.**

4 In Greece and Cyprus telephone numbers tend to be given in two-digit pairs. Listen to Costas giving us his telephone number, 56 01 72. Now practise saying these numbers from his diary, checking them with your audio.

> Eleni 35 88 93   Vangelis 52 69 00
>
> Anna 27 14 60   Maria 86 41 87
>
> Stella 77 10 11   Nikos 22 03 21

5 Practise pronouncing these Greek and Cypriot place names, then check your pronunciation with the audio. Don't forget to stress the part of the word with the accent over it.

Θεσσαλονίκη	**Κεφαλονιά**	**Λευκωσία**
Ζάκυνθος	**Χαλκιδική**	**Λεμεσός**
Αίγινα	**Πελοπόννησος**	**Δελφοί**
Ναύπλιο	**Κέρκυρα**	**Ολυμπία**

Do you know the English versions of these place names?

6 Look at the information on the following holiday survey form. Can you say which questions this person was asked to obtain this information? Note that Greeks often write their surname before their first name. Check the full dialogue in the *Audio scripts and answers*.

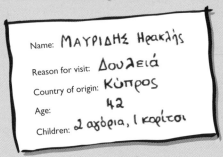

> Name: ΜΑΥΡΙΔΗΣ Ηρακλής
>
> Reason for visit: Δουλειά
>
> Country of origin: Κύπρος
>
> Age: 42
>
> Children: 2 αγόρια, 1 κορίτσι

Did you notice that when someone says they are from Cyprus, the final **ς** is left off **Κύπρος**? ('**Είμαι από την Κύπρο.**')

7 Fill in the missing infomation about Heracles from the form on the previous page. Then listen and answer the questions about him. Note that **Έχει** means '**He/She** has'.

Τον λένε .... Μαυρίδη. Είναι εδώ για .... Είναι από την .... Είναι .... χρονών. Έχει τρία παιδιά, δύο .... και ένα ....

8 In the Wordsearch below, can you find the ten words listed? All describe drinks and snacks you may wish to order in Greek.

Σ	Π	Ε	Ψ	Ο	Μ	Χ	Γ	Θ	Α	Ζ
Κ	Δ	Α	Ρ	Ε	Σ	Υ	Λ	Ι	Λ	Μ
Ε	Ε	Φ	Γ	Δ	Μ	Π	Υ	Ρ	Α	Ν
Τ	Α	Ο	Μ	Ω	Ρ	Δ	Κ	Λ	Ψ	Ο
Ο	Γ	Λ	Υ	Π	Τ	Α	Ο	Ε	Θ	Μ
Κ	Ζ	Ν	Χ	Ζ	Α	Ο	Σ	Μ	Τ	Π
Ο	Α	Ω	Ν	Κ	Ο	Α	Ν	Ο	Ξ	Α
Κ	Μ	Ε	Τ	Ρ	Ι	Ο	Ε	Ν	Ψ	Α
Ω	Π	Δ	Υ	Γ	Ν	Ε	Ρ	Α	Θ	Υ
Ξ	Ο	Ψ	Ρ	Ι	Α	Χ	Λ	Δ	Ζ	Η
Τ	Ν	Ε	Ι	Κ	Β	Τ	Γ	Α	Λ	Α

μέτριο
γλυκό
γάλα
σκέτο
λεμονάδα
μπύρα
ούζο
τυρί
ζαμπόν
παγωτό

9 What changes would you make to the following if speaking to someone in an informal situation?

α **Γειά σας!**
β **Πώς σας λένε;**
γ **Από πού είσαστε;**
δ **Αυτός είναι ο άντρας σας;**
ε **Έχετε παιδιά;**
ζ **Τι κάνετε;**

Γειά σας!

Πώς σας λένε;

10 Look at the menu from the **Καφετερία Καλλιθέα**. Can you say how much the following items cost?

α an English breakfast β an instant coffee γ a cheese sandwich
δ a lemonade ε a soda water ζ a cheese pie η a whisky
θ a baklava

ΚΑΦΕΤΕΡΙΑ ΚΑΛΛΙΘΕΑ

Ελληνικός καφές .... € 1,70	Τυρόπιττα .... € 1,20
Νεσκαφέ .... € 2,20	Τοστ/Σάντουϊτς με:
Καπουτσίνο .... € 2,40	ζαμπόν .... € 1,60
Σοκολάτα ζεστή .... € 2	τυρί .... € 1,60
Τσάι .... € 2,10	Ομελέτα .... € 4
Λεμονάδα .... € 1,50	Μπρέκφαστ αγγλικό .... € 6
Σόδα .... € 1,40	Μπρέκφαστ κοντινεντάλ .... € 3
Κοκακόλα .... € 1,50	Γιαούρτι με μέλι .... € 3,40
Χυμός πορτοκάλι ... € 1,80	Πίτσα (ατομική) .... € 4,40
Μπύρα .... € 2,80	Κανταΐφι .... € 2,50
Ούζο .... € 2	Μπακλαβάς .... € 2,50
Ουίσκυ .... € 4,60	Παγωτό .... € 3,60
Μεταξά .... € 3,50	Πάστες .... € 2,80

11 Listen to a customer ordering items from the menu for himself and three friends. Work out how much his bill will come to. Listen for the waiter saying **άλλο;** which means '(anything) else?'

12 Practise ordering some snacks and drinks from the menu using the different expressions learnt in Unit 4. Remember to use **ένα** or **μία** as appropriate.

5 πέντε

Υπάρχει
τράπεζα εδώ;

- asking what facilities are available
  . . . and how to find them
- understanding basic directions
  . . . and asking for help to understand

στην Ελλάδα και στην Κύπρο . . .

many small places do not have tourist information offices, and so the **περίπτερο** (kiosk) is particularly useful. This is a characteristic feature of Greek and Cypriot towns and villages, selling everything from cigarettes and newspapers to confectionery and razors, and the owner is often an excellent source of information. Most large towns and villages will also have at least one **(ίντερ)νετ καφέ** (internet café).

43

Asking what facilities are available . . .

I Listen to these key phrases.

Συγνώμη	Excuse me
Υπάρχει τράπεζα εδώ;	Is there a bank here?
Υπάρχει φαρμακείο εδώ	There's a chemist's here
Δεν υπάρχει ξενοδοχείο εδώ	There isn't a hotel here
Είναι εδώ / εκεί	It's here / there

στα Ελληνικά . . .

the word for 'a' is not required before place words in statements and questions such as those in the key phrases.

2 You'll find the following in most towns in Greece and Cyprus. Can you match the Greek words with the English?

α **Σουπερμάρκετ**
β **Φαρμακείο**
γ **Τουαλέτα**
δ **Μουσείο**
ε **Τηλέφωνο**
ζ **Εκκλησία**

Chemist's
Toilet
Church
Supermarket
Museum
Telephone

3 Listen to three visitors making enquiries at a **περίπτερο** about some of the facilities above. Indicate by ticking **Ναι** or **Όχι** whether the statements below are true. **Συγνώμη** also means 'I'm sorry'.

		Ναι	**Όχι**
α	there's a telephone		
β	there's a chemist's		
γ	there's a museum		
δ	there's a church		

. . . and how to find them

4 Listen to these key phrases.

Πού είναι . . .	Where is . . .
. . . ο φούρνος;	. . . the baker's?
. . . η πλατεία;	. . . the square?
. . . το ταχυδρομείο;	. . . the post office?
Θα πάτε ίσια	Go straight on
Θα πάτε δεξιά	Go right
Θα στρίψετε αριστερά	Turn left

στα Ελληνικά . . .

all nouns fall into one of three genders. Each gender has a different word for 'the': masculine **ο**, feminine **η**, neuter **το**.
You can usually tell the gender of a noun by its ending:

-ος (m.),	**ο φούρνος**	baker's		
-α or **-η** (f.),	**η πλατεία**	square	**η φίλη**	female friend
-ο or **-ι** (n.).	**το μουσείο**	museum	**το λιμάνι**	harbour

'Borrowed' words, such as **το σουπερμάρκετ** (the supermarket), are generally neuter.

5 Which word for 'the' is needed for the following places?

___ τράπεζα	___ περίπτερο
___ ξενοδοχείο	___ τηλέφωνο
___ φαρμακείο	___ τουαλέτα
___ εκκλησία	___ μουσείο

6 Listen as Eleni asks for directions, then answer the questions below. You will hear the word **μετά**, which means 'then'.

- Where does Eleni want to go?
- Which is the first direction given to her?
- What should she do after turning right?

Understanding basic directions . . .

1   Listen to these key phrases.

Είναι . . .	It's . . .
. . . κοντά / μακριά	. . . near / far
. . . δεξιά / αριστερά	. . . on the right / left
100 μέτρα από 'δω	100 metres from here

2   Pam is being given directions from the station, to the hotel, the bank and the chemist's. Listen, and label the boxes (marked 1 to 3) on the map. As you hear each one decide which number it is on the map.

3   Now listen to this conversation between a visitor and a passer-by and answer the questions below. **μόνο** means 'only'.

- Where does the visitor want to go?
- Is it near or far?
- How far is it?

4   How would you ask for directions to:

- the post office
- the baker's
- the toilet?

... and asking for help to understand

5 Listen to these key phrases.

Δεν κατάλαβα	I didn't understand
Το λέτε πιο αργά;	(Can you) say it more slowly?
Το λέτε ξανά παρακαλώ;	(Can you) say it again please?

6 Listen to Petros asking a passer-by for directions. Note the word order of the phrase **εδώ κοντά** meaning 'near here', or 'nearby'.

  a Where does Petros want to go?

  β Why can't he go there?

  γ What is the alternative suggested?

  δ After being given directions, what does he ask the passer-by?

  ε Trace the route on the map below that Petros must take. Can you say which number he should arrive at?

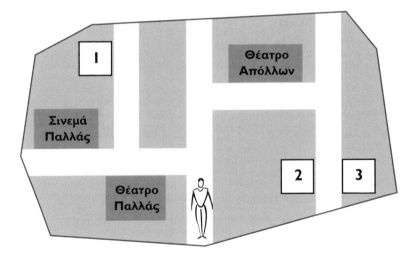

7 Look at the map again and listen to Petros being given directions by three different people to the **Θέατρο Παλλάς** (Pallas Theatre). Which person gives the correct directions according to your map?

Put it all together

1 Look at the places in the box. Using the phrases in the speech bubbles can you say whether there is or isn't one of them in your home town?

bank
kiosk
church
hotel
museum
post office

2 Match the Greek phrases with the English.

α	**Είναι κοντά;**	It isn't far
β	**Είναι δεξιά**	It's on the right
γ	**Θα στρίψετε αριστερά**	Go straight on
δ	**Είναι εδώ κοντά**	Is it near?
ε	**Δεν είναι μακριά**	Turn left
ζ	**Δεν θα πάτε αριστερά**	It's near here
η	**Θα πάτε ίσια**	Don't go left

3 You consult your phrase book to find the Greek words for the places in English listed below – but the book doesn't indicate which word to use for 'the'. Work out the right form and use it to practise asking:
Πού είναι . . . ; ('Where is the . . . ?')

sea	__ **θάλασσα**	clinic	__ **κλινική**
hospital	__ **νοσοκομείο**	station	__ **σταθμός**
monastery	__ **μοναστήρι**	seafront	__ **παραλία**
garage	__ **γκαράζ**	restaurant	__ **εστιατόριο**

Now you're talking!

I   In the hotel you ask the receptionist for some local information.

◆ Greet her and ask if there's a restaurant nearby.

◇ **Ναι, το Εστιατόριο Άργος.**

◆ Ask her if it's far away.

◇ **Όχι, μόνο πενήντα μέτρα. Θα στρίψετε δεξιά και μετά ξανά δεξιά.**

◆ You didn't quite catch that; ask her to repeat it.

◇ **Θα στρίψετε δεξιά και μετά ξανά δεξιά.**

◆ Thank her and ask her where the lift (**το ασανσέρ**) is.

◇ **Είναι εκεί, αριστερά.**

2   Later, in the restaurant you ask the waiter some questions. Here the waiter uses **στο περίπτερο** to mean both 'to the kiosk' and 'at the kiosk'. You need to know how to:

◆ call the waiter and ask him if there's a telephone

◆ say you didn't understand and ask him to say it more slowly

◆ thank him and ask where the toilet is.

3   Finally, you go to **το τουριστικό γραφείο** (the tourist office) for directions to:

the hospital ▨▨▨   the garage ▨▨▨
the station ▨▨▨   the seafront ▨▨▨

After taking part in the conversation listen again and draw an arrow in each box to indicate whether you should turn right, turn left or go straight on.

Quiz

1 How would you ask 'Is there a supermarket/restaurant/kiosk/garage here?'?
2 What word would you use after **εδώ** to mean 'near here'?
3 How would you ask 'Is it far?'?
4 Which word for 'the' is used with these Greek words?
  ___ **σταθμός** / ___ **σουπερμάρκετ** / ___ **τράπεζα**
5 If someone said **Θα στρίψετε δεξιά** would you turn left or right?
6 How would you make **το περίπτερο** mean 'at/to the kiosk'?
7 What Greek word means 'then' or 'after'?
8 How would you ask someone to repeat something?
9 Can you ask where these places are?
  the museum, the church, the Hotel Omega, the tourist office
10 How do you change **δεν κατάλαβα** to mean 'I understood'?

Now check whether you can . . .

■ ask and say what there is and is not in the area

■ ask where certain places are

■ ask if a place is near or far

■ say if you have or haven't understood something

■ give and understand some basic directions

■ ask someone to repeat something or say it more slowly

To help you remember the Greek you learn, bring it into your everyday life as much as you can. Practise saying what there is and isn't in your home town, using the places and buildings you see around you as stimuli to help you remember the Greek names for them. When in Greece or Cyprus take every opportunity to speak Greek and don't be frightened to ask someone to repeat something or speak more slowly.

6 Πού μένετε;

- talking about where you live
  . . . and work
- finding out where places are
  . . . and when they are open

στην Ελλάδα και στην Κύπρο . . .

when telling someone where you live, it's useful, if possible, to be able to relate the place to a well-known town or city, for example one with a famous football team!

In working towns, shops and offices tend to open early in the mornings and, because of the heat at midday, close in the afternoons, when a long 'siesta' period is taken. Most of them will then re-open in the early evenings for two to three hours on certain days. In tourist places, they have longer opening hours.

Talking about where you live . . .

| Listen to these key phrases.

Πού μένετε / μένεις;	Where do you live? (formal / informal)
Μένω . . .	I live . . .
. . . στο Λονδίνο	. . . in London
. . . στη Λευκωσία	. . . in Nicosia
. . . στην Αθήνα	. . . in Athens

στα Ελληνικά . . .

● 'the' is used with place names, **ο Καναδάς** (Canada), **η Αθήνα, το Λονδίνο.**

● After **σε** (in, to, at, on), **από** (from), and **για** (for):
   the word for 'the' with masculine and feminine nouns changes:
   ο (m.) ➔ **το(ν)**   **η** (f.) ➔ **τη(ν)**
   το (n.) doesn't change.

● A final **ν** is added (**τον, την**) if the noun begins with any vowel or one of the letters **κ, π** or **τ**.

● When **σε** is followed by **το(ν)** or **τη(ν)**, the two words combine:
   σε + το(ν) = στο(ν)   **σε + τη(ν) = στη(ν)**
   σε + το = στο

2 Listen as Thanassis talks about himself. Then fill the gaps below with the appropriate missing word. Note **αλλά**, meaning 'but'.

● **Πού μένεις, Θανάση;**
● **Μένω εδώ ____ Ναύπλιο, αλλά είμαι από ____ Άγια Νάπα ____ Κύπρο.**

3 Work out the identities of the cities below. Then use the lists to practise saying where people live and where they come from.

e.g. **Ο Simon μένει στην Οξφόρδη, και η Carmen είναι από τη Μαδρίτη.**

Simon	**η Οξφόρδη**	Carmen	**η Μαδρίτη**
Maureen	**το Εδιμβούργο**	Burt	**η Νέα Υόρκη**
Kylie	**η Μελβούρνη**	Fritz	**το Βερολίνο**
Patrick	**το Δουβλίνο**	Monique	**το Παρίσι**

. . . and work

4 Listen to these key phrases.

Πού δουλεύετε / δουλεύεις;	Where do you work? (formal / informal)
Δουλεύω σε γραφείο / μαγαζί*	I work in an office / shop
Δουλεύει για . . .	He/She works for . . .
. . . το Ταχυδρομείο	. . . the Post Office
. . . τη British Airways	. . . British Airways

*Note from the example above, that Greek does not use the word for 'a/an' with **σε** in these expressions.

στα Ελληνικά . . .

to show *who* is doing something you change the ending of the verb. You generally need only use the words **εγώ** (I), **εσύ/εσείς** (you), **αυτός** (he), **αυτή** (she) etc. for clarity or emphasis.

	(to) live/stay	(to) work	(to) do
(εγώ)	μένω	δουλεύω	κάνω
(εσύ)	μένεις	δουλεύεις	κάνεις
(εσείς)	μένετε	δουλεύετε	κάνετε
(αυτός / αυτή)	μένει	δουλεύει	κάνει

---

5 Manolis asks Kiki, Pavlos and Loula where they work. Listen, then write the person's name under the appropriate workplace.

σχολείο	νοσοκομείο	SONY
school	hospital	

Name ....

6 Listen to Maro asking Antonis where he works and answer the questions below. Listen for the word **τώρα**, meaning 'now'.

α Who works in Larissa? β Who doesn't work now?
γ Where does Antonis live?

Finding out where places are . . .

1   Listen to these key phrases.

Είναι . . .	It's . . .
. . . δίπλα στο λιμάνι	. . . next to the harbour
. . . κοντά στην πλατεία	. . . near the square
. . . μακριά από το κέντρο	. . . a long way from the centre
. . . απέναντι από την εκκλησία	. . . opposite the church

2   Listen to visitors asking where certain places are and complete the sentences.

    α   The Hotel Olga is .... the museum.
    β   The church is .... the square.
    γ   The chemist's is .... the cinema.

3   Look at the map and complete the sentences below using the relevant location expressions from the key phrases.

    α   **Υπάρχει εστιατόριο** .... **παραλία.**
    β   **Η τράπεζα είναι** .... **ξενοδοχείο.**
    γ   **Υπάρχει φαρμακείο** .... **νοσοκομείο.**
    δ   **Το μουσείο είναι** .... **λιμάνι.**

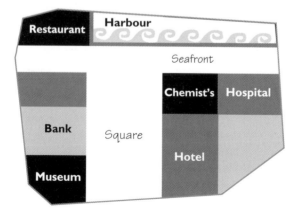

. . . and when they are open

1 Listen to these key phrases.

Τι ώρα ανοίγει;	What time does it open?
Τι ώρα κλείνει;	What time does it close?
Ανοίγει / Κλείνει στις . . .	It opens / closes at . . .
. . . (οχτώ) η ώρα	. . . (eight) o'clock
. . . (δύο) και μισή	. . . half past (two)

2 Listen and note the opening and closing times of these places.

		ανοίγει	**κλείνει**
α	shop	....	....
β	restaurant	....	....
γ	garage	....	....

στα Ελληνικά . . .

when telling the time, the numbers 1, 3 and 4 change to:

1 → **μία**   3 → **τρεις**   4 → **τέσσερις**

- a quarter <u>past</u> 5 is **πέντε <u>και</u> τέταρτο** literally '5 <u>and</u> a quarter'
- a quarter <u>to</u> 5 is **πέντε <u>παρά</u> τέταρτο** literally '5 <u>but for</u> a quarter'

3 Listen to these people asking what time it is – **Τι ώρα είναι;**
Then draw the correct times on the blank clock faces.

4 Now practise saying what time it is from these clock faces:

α 2:45   β 4:30   γ 1:15

Put it all together

1 Match the Greek with the English.

α **δουλεύω**   it opens
β **είναι**   you live (informal)
γ **κάνετε**   she is
δ **μένεις**   he has
ε **έχει**   I work
ζ **ανοίγει**   you do (formal)

2 Underline the correct alternative in each sentence.

α **Δουλεύω** στο/σε **γραφείο.**
β **Η Σοφία μένει δίπλα** στην/στον **εκκλησία.**
γ **Ο Μανώλης δουλεύει** για τη/στη **Sony.**
δ **Ο σταθμός είναι μακριά** στο/από το **κέντρο.**
ε **Είσαστε** από τη/από την **Αθήνα;**

3 Look at the notices below, and practise telling a Greek visitor about the opening and closing times shown as in the following example.

e.g. **Η τράπεζα ανοίγει στις εννιά και μισή και κλείνει στις τέσσερις και μισή.**

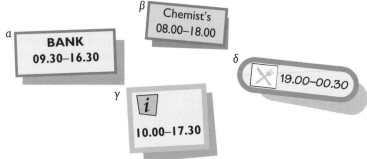

Note that although the 24-hour clock may be used on notices or timetables, it is rarely used in spoken Greek.

Now you're talking!

I   Imagine you are Susan Lord, at your first meeting with Daphne, a Greek visitor you have been asked to show round York. You can use the informal form.

   ◆ First, greet Daphne and introduce yourself to her.
   ◇ **Καλημέρα Σούζαν. Μένεις εδώ;**
   ◆ Say yes, you live here in York.
   ◇ **Πού δουλεύεις;**
   ◆ Reply that you work in a tourist office in Leeds.
   ◇ **Το Λητς είναι μακριά από 'δω;**
   ◆ Say no, it's very near.

2   Daphne wants to know where the bank is, and what time it opens. Listen for her questions, then tell her that:

   ◆ the bank is next to the Ritz Cinema, opposite the church.
   ◆ it opens at 9.30 and closes at 5.00.

3   Find out some more about Daphne. You'll need to know how to:

   ◆ ask her where she lives
   ◆ ask her if it's near Athens
   ◆ ask if she works in Veria.

4   A Greek visitor asks you about yourself. Prepare your answers and then be guided by the audio. This time use the formal form. You'll need to know how to say:

   ◆ which town you live in and where it is
   ◆ whether you live in the town centre or not
   ◆ whether you work or not, giving relevant details if appropriate.

Quiz

1 To ask someone where they live, do you say **Πού μένω;** or **Πού μένετε;**?
2 Is 'in an office' **στην γραφείο**, **στο γραφείο** or **σε γραφείο**?
3 Fill in the missing letters to find three places in town:
   τ - - - - ρ - - - - ο / **φ - - - α - - - ο** / **ε - - - α - - - - ο**.
4 Is 'opposite the' **απέναντι από το** or **δίπλα στο**?
5 Which word for 'in (the)' would you use for the following?
   .... **Λονδίνο** / .... **Κρήτη** / .... **Νέα Υόρκη**
6 Can you complete the following?
   Το μαγαζί κλείνει .... **δέκα η ώρα**.
7 How would you say you work for Ford?
8 Is **δουλεύει** or **δουλεύετε** the correct verb for this sentence?
   Ο φίλος μου .... **μακριά από 'δω**.

Now check whether you can . . .

■ ask someone where they live and work

■ say where you live and work

■ understand where one place is in relation to another

■ ask what time a place opens and closes

■ understand when someone tells you the time

As you become more familiar with the Greek alphabet you might like to start using a phrase book, or a simple dictionary, to supplement the vocabulary in this course. Look for phrases which are relevant to your life, and your situation. For example, if you work in a college and you find that the word for college is **κολλέγιο**, you can say: **Δουλεύω σε κολλέγιο**. Why not compile your own vocabulary book to note down new words and phrases as you come across them? This will help your learning process.

Πόσο κάνει;

- asking for something in a shop
- saying how much you want
- asking the price of something
- understanding amounts

στην Ελλάδα και στην Κύπρο . . .

local people tend to shop daily for fresh produce which is available at the street market (**η λαϊκή αγορά**), or from the back of a truck, as well as in the shops. You may see shop signs written in an older form of Greek, not used in the modern, everyday, spoken language. Some examples are: **ΟΠΩΡΟΠΩΛΕΙΟΝ** (fruit seller) selling both **φρούτα** (fruit) and **λαχανικά** (vegetables), **ΙΧΘΥΟΠΩΛΕΙΟΝ** (fish seller) selling **ψάρια** (fish), and **ΑΡΤΟΠΩΛΕΙΟΝ** (bread seller) selling **ψωμί** (bread).

The unit of currency in Greece is the euro (**το ευρώ**). In Cyprus it is currently the pound (**η λίρα**), for which the **£** sign is used. However, it is expected that Cyprus will soon join the EU and adopt the euro.

59

Asking for something in a shop

1 Listen to these key phrases.

Τι θέλετε; / Ορίστε;	What do you want? / Yes?
Θέλω μία εφημερίδα	I want a newspaper
(Μήπως) έχετε ψωμί / κάρτες;	Do you (happen to) have any bread / cards?
Ναι, έχουμε	Yes, we have
Δυστυχώς δεν έχουμε	Unfortunately we haven't

2 Kiriakos is preparing his shopping list. Listen and tick the items you hear. Which items has he forgotten?

butter	**βούτυρο**	▨	biscuits	**μπισκότα**	▨
grapes	**σταφύλια**	▨	jam	**μαρμελάδα**	▨
cigarettes	**τσιγάρα**	▨	cards	**κάρτες**	▨
aspirins	**ασπιρίνες**	▨	tomatoes	**ντομάτες**	▨
stamps	**γραμματόσημα**	▨	yoghurt	**γιαούρτι**	▨

στα Ελληνικά . . .

you form plurals by changing word endings:
- masculine nouns: **-ος → -οι**
- feminine nouns: **-α** and **-η → -ες**
- neuter nouns: **-ι → -ια** and **-ο → -α**.

3 How would you ask for more than one of these?

εφημερίδα	newspaper	**βιβλίο**	book
ελιά	olive	**σάκος**	holdall
καρπούζι	watermelon	**τηλεκάρτα**	telephone card
μήλο	apple	**πορτοκάλι**	orange

Saying how much you want

1 Listen to these key phrases.

Πόσο / Πόσα θέλετε;	How much / many do you want?
Θέλω . . .	I want . . .
. . . ένα κιλό φέτα	. . . a kilo of feta
. . . μισό κιλό λεμόνια	. . . ½ kilo of lemons
. . . ένα τέταρτο σταφύλια	. . . ¼ kilo of grapes
Θέλετε τίποτ' άλλο;	Do you want anything else?

2 Listen as Kiriakos does his shopping. How much or how many of the following items does he want?

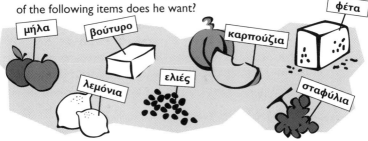

στα Ελληνικά . . .

the word 'of' in phrases like 'a kilo of ' etc. is not translated.

Τρία (3) and **τέσσερα** (4) change to **τρεις** and **τέσσερις** with masculine and feminine words.

3 Kiriakos now goes to the **περίπτερο** for three items.

- What does he ask for? How many does he want of each?
- Which three phrases does he use to ask for them?

4 At the general groceries store (**ΠΑΝΤΟΠΩΛΕΙΟΝ**) ask for the goods on this list.

> ¼ kilo feta cheese
> 3 beers
> 4 yoghurts
> ½ kilo butter
> 1 phonecard

Asking the price of something

1 Listen to these key phrases.

Πόσο κάνει . . .;	How much is . . . / it?
Πόσο κάνουνε . . .;	How much are . . . / they?
αυτό / αυτά;	this / these?
Κάνει 4 ευρώ	It's 4 euros
Κάνουνε 8 λίρες	They are £8

2 Zoë is shopping in Cyprus. Listen and identify which items she asks the price of. Which item is not mentioned at all?

- **φιλμ** (camera) film
- **καπέλο** hat
- **ομπρέλα** (beach) umbrella
- **μπουκάλι νερό** bottle of water
- **αντηλιακό** sun-tan lotion
- **σαγιονάρες** 'flip-flops'

στα Ελληνικά . . .

there are plural forms for 'the':

	m.	f.	n.
singular	ο	η	το
plural	οι	οι	τα

---

3 You want to know the cost of the gifts (**τα δώρα**) below, but you don't know the Greek words. First, practise asking the price of each item, using **Πόσο κάνει αυτό;** or **Πόσο κάνουνε αυτά;**

- plates (**πιάτα**)
- picture or icon (**εικόνα**)
- holdalls (**σάκοι**)
- set of worry beads (**κομπολόϊ**)

Practise again, this time using the Greek words for the gifts. You'll need to work out the word for 'the'.

Understanding amounts

I Listen to these key phrases.

Πόσο κάνει ή πετσέτα;   How much is the towel?
Πόσο κάνουνε τα σπίρτα;   How much are the matches?
Κάνει € 5,60   It is / costs €5.60
Κάνουνε 15 λεπτά   They are / cost €0.15

Greece is the only European country to use a different word for the euro cent **λεπτό / λεπτά** (also the Greek word for minute/s). This could be due to the fact that the word 'cent' is used for the smaller units of the Cypriot pound. Note that the written form of the euro uses a comma to separate the digits whereas English uses a decimal point.

2 You are shopping for a Greek friend. Listen to the shopkeeper adding up your purchases. Fill in the price of each item as you hear it mentioned. Listen for **τα φιλμ** (the films); 'borrowed' words don't change in the plural.

I	**τηλεκάρτα**	....	5 **φιλμ**	....
2	**τσιγάρα**	....	6 **σοκολάτες**	....
3	**τσάι**	....	7 **Νεσκαφέ**	....
4	**ασπιρίνες**	....	8 **μπύρες**	....

                 όλα μαζί (altogether) ....

3 Back home you tell your friend how much each item cost. Practise saying the prices aloud, and check by listening to the audio again.

4 At the post office you overhear a woman asking for stamps. Here, **αυτά** means 'that's all'.

● How does she ask the price of a stamp for England?
● How many does she buy?

Put it all together

1 Match the English with the Greek phrases.

1	Do you have any . . .?	α	**Μήπως έχετε . . .;**
2	How much are those?	β	**Πόσο κάνει;**
3	Do you happen to have . . .?	γ	**Θέλω . . .**
4	How much is it?	δ	**Έχετε . . .;**
5	I want . . .	ε	**Πόσο κάνουνε αυτά;**

2 If you buy three items each costing the following amounts, and pay for them all with a 50 euro note, how much change would you expect?

- **τριάντα δύο ευρώ**
- **οχτώ και πενήντα**
- **ένα ευρώ και εβδομήντα πέντε λεπτά**

3 Below is a list of the things you want to buy for a beach picnic. Imagine yourself asking for them in a shop which sells fruit, vegetables and general groceries – the **ΟΠΩΡΟΠΑΝΤΟΠΩΛΕΙΟΝ**. Can you remember the various ways of asking for things?

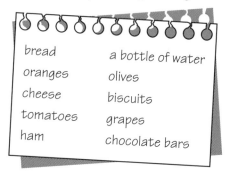

bread

oranges

cheese

tomatoes

ham

a bottle of water

olives

biscuits

grapes

chocolate bars

4 You will want to stock up your fridge with essentials at the beginning of your holiday. Write out your shopping list in Greek using items from this unit.

"Now you're talking!

1   On arrival at your holiday apartment you decide to take your list of essential groceries to the **ΟΠΩΡΟΠΑΝΤΟΠΩΛΕΙΟΝ**.

The shopkeeper greets you.

◇ **Καλημέρα, τι θέλετε;**
◆ Ask for a watermelon and a kilo of apples.
◇ **Ορίστε, τίποτ' άλλο;**
◆ Ask whether he has any olives.
◇ **Δυστυχώς, δεν έχουμε.**
◆ Say OK.

2   Next, to the grocery section . . .

◆ Ask how much the butter is.
◇ **Κάνει πέντε και εξήντα.**
◆ Ask for half a kilo and six yoghurts.
◇ **Θέλετε τίποτ' άλλο;**
◆ Say yes, you want a bottle of milk and a jar of jam (just say 'one jam').
◇ **Ορίστε. Αυτά;**
◆ Say, yes that's all. Ask how much it costs altogether.

3   Then you go to the **περίπτερο** for some other items. Read the following notes then be guided by the audio. You will need to be able to:

◆ ask if they have any aspirins
◆ ask how much a stamp for Ireland costs
◆ say you want three stamps for Ireland and one for America.

Quiz

1 How would you ask in Greek: 'How much are the lemons?'?
2 Would you ask for **τρεις** or **τρία κιλά ντομάτες**?
3 How much is **εκατόν είκοσι δύο ευρώ και ενενήντα έξι λεπτά**?
4 What is the unit of currency in Cyprus?
5 How would you find out if a shop has cigarettes?
6 How would you say 'How much is this?'?
7 Would a shopkeeper say: **Πόσο καφέ θέλετε;** or **Πόσα καφέ θέλετε;**?
8 What is the Greek word that means both a euro cent and a minute?
9 What are the plural forms of these words?
   η κάρτα / το μπισκότο / το φιλμ / το καρπούζι
10 In Cyprus, how would you ask for a stamp for Greece?

Now check whether you can . . .

■ ask whether a shop has a certain item or items

■ say you want something and how much/many

■ ask the price of various items

■ understand prices in euros and Cypriot pounds

It's a good idea to learn a noun together with the appropriate word for 'the'; **το μήλο** (the apple). Try listing new words in gender groups in your vocabulary book. In this way you will become more familiar with the gender patterns of nouns and notice some exceptions, e.g. **το γάλα** (milk).

However, when speaking to Greek people, don't worry too much about getting the gender right. They will still understand you if you use the wrong word for 'the'. It is more important to say something, even if slightly incorrectly, than to say nothing at all!

Έλεγχος! 2

I Can you identify the places where you would be likely to hear the enquiries and requests below?

ΦΑΡΜΑΚΕΙΟ ☐   ΣΟΥΠΕΡΜΑΡΚΕΤ ☐   ΠΕΡΙΠΤΕΡΟ ■

ΚΑΦΕΤΕΡΙΑ ☐   ΤΡΑΠΕΖΑ ■   ΤΑΧΥΔΡΟΜΕΙΟ ☐

α **Τι εφημερίδα θέλετε;**
β **Μήπως έχετε λίρες;**
γ **Θέλω δύο μπύρες παρακαλώ.**
δ **Πόσο κάνουνε οι ασπιρίνες;**
ε **Συγνώμη, πού είναι τα μπισκότα;**
ζ **Πόσο κάνει ένα γραμματόσημο για την Αγγλία;**

2 Listen to a tourist guide giving information about local places. Then read the statements below and correct any wrong information.

α The museum is near the square. It opens at 10.00 and closes at 4.30.
β Saint George's monastery is next to the church, 100 metres away.
γ For the tourist office, go straight on and turn right at the cinema. It's there on the left.

3 Match a word from list A with one from list B.

A		B	
1	**αριστερά**	α	**νοσοκομείο**
2	**γραμματόσημο**	β	**ομπρέλα**
3	**θάλασσα**	γ	**δεξιά**
4	**ανοίγει**	δ	**παραλία**
5	**μήλα**	ε	**εβδομήντα**
6	**εκατό**	ζ	**ταχυδρομείο**
7	**καπέλο**	η	**καρπούζι**
8	**κλινική**	θ	**κλείνει**

4 Can you rearrange the words below to form complete sentences?

a αριστερά / Η / από / είναι / τράπεζα / ξενοδοχείο / το

β Θέλω / κιλό / ένα / τυρί / μισό / παρακαλώ / και / καρπούζι

γ μέτρα / είναι / θέατρο / από / εδώ / Το / εκατό

5 Which of the phrases on the right would you use . . .

a	when you'd like to hear something again?	1	Το λέτε ξανά παρακαλώ;
β	to ask where the telephone is?	2	Πιο αργά, παρακαλώ
γ	to attract someone's attention?	3	Συγνώμη!
δ	when someone is speaking too quickly?	4	Δεν κατάλαβα
ε	to say you didn't understand?	5	Υπάρχει τουαλέτα;
ζ	to ask if there's a toilet?	6	Πού είναι το τηλέφωνο;

6 You can solve the puzzle below by following the clues to finding the right Greek words. Write them down in capital letters.

a Not there, but ....

β To say what you want . . .

γ . . . and to say where you work.

δ The shop opens at eight and .... at two.

ε A religious venue.

ζ 10.15 is **δέκα και** ....

η On the other side.

θ A daily read.

ι More than one night?

κ A capital place to be?

The word in the vertical column is the name of a group of Greek islands.

7 First work out how to ask the price of the goods on your shopping
list. Then listen to the correct answers and fill them in below.

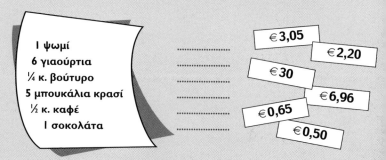

1 ψωμί
6 γιαούρτια
¼ κ. βούτυρο
5 μπουκάλια κρασί
½ κ. καφέ
1 σοκολάτα

€3,05
€2,20
€30
€6,96
€0,65
€0,50

8 Now work out the total cost of the shopping in Activity 7 and decide
which of the following amounts is correct.

α **σαράντα πέντε ευρώ και τριάντα έξι λεπτά**

β **σαράντα τρία ευρώ και τριάντα έξι λεπτά**

γ **σαράντα τρία ευρώ και σαράντα έξι λεπτά**

9 Listen to the eight questions on your audio. Pause the audio after each
one and decide which of these answers is the right one. Number them
1 to 8.

Νούμερο

α **Όχι, αυτά.**

β **Εβδομήντα πέντε λεπτά το κιλό.**

γ **Όχι, στην Αγγλία.**

δ **Στις πέντε.**

ε **Δυστυχώς έχω μόνο ψωμί.**

ζ **Μισό κιλό.**

η **Στην Αθήνα.**

θ **Θα στρίψετε αριστερά εδώ.**

10　Read this extract from a local Greek newspaper. Then answer **ναι** or **όχι** to the following statements about the article.

Τον λένε Στηβ Τέϊλορ. Είναι σαράντα χρονών και είναι Άγγλος από το Λονδίνο. Δουλεύει για τον Ο.Τ.Ε. στη Λαμία και μένει εκεί κοντά με τη γυναίκα του. Έχει δύο παιδιά. Το χόμπυ του είναι το γκολφ.

> ο **Ο.Τ.Ε.** = Greek Telecommunications Organization
>
> η **γυναίκα του** = *his* wife (see Grammar, no. 5)

		Ναι / Όχι	
α	Steve is an Englishman living in Greece.	☐	☐
β	He lives and works in Lamia.	☐	☐
γ	He is married with two children.	☐	☐
δ	He is thirty years old.	☐	☐
ε	His hobby is golf.	☐	☐

11　How would Steve describe himself? Here is the same article with some words omitted. Fill in the gaps below as if you were Steve speaking.

.... **λένε Στηβ Τέϊλορ.** .... **σαράντα χρονών, και** .... **Άγγλος από το Λονδίνο.** .... **για τον Ο.Τ.Ε. στη Λαμία και** .... **εκεί κοντά με τη γυναίκα μου.** .... **δυο παιδιά. Το χόμπυ** .... **είναι το γκολφ.**

8

Θέλω ένα δωμάτιο

- checking in at reception
- finding a hotel room
- booking ahead
- making requests

στην Ελλάδα και στην Κύπρο . . .

hotels range mainly from luxury class to C **(Γ)** class (basic), but many visitors prefer to stay in 'village rooms'; you may see signs saying **ΕΝΟΙΚΙΑΖΟΝΤΑΙ ΔΩΜΑΤΙΑ** (Rooms to Rent). The accommodation varies from a simple room with shared facilities, to an apartment (**διαμέρισμα**) with its own bathroom (**μπάνιο**). Owned by local people, these village rooms can be the ideal choice of accommodation for students of Greek who wish to practise the spoken language as the owners are usually ready to pass the time of day in conversation with their guests.

Checking in at reception

1 Listen to these key phrases.

Έχω κλείσει ένα δωμάτιο	I've booked a room
... στο ισόγειο	... on the ground floor
... στον πρώτο όροφο	... on the first floor
... στο δεύτερο όροφο	... on the second floor
Το όνομά σας;	Your name?
Το διαβατήριό σας παρακαλώ	Your passport please

2 Athina, the receptionist at the **Ξενοδοχείο Ζευς** in Athens, greets some guests, checks their names in the register and gives them their keys (**το κλειδί – τα κλειδιά**). Listen several times and fill in the details on the hotel register. Note how, in formal situations, people often give their surname first.

Name	How many rooms	Room number(s)	Which floor
Κύριος Παυλίδης			
Μακρή Σοφία			
Ιωαννίδης Στέφανος			

3 One of the guests is Cypriot and Athina asks for a passport. Can you say which guest it is?

Finding a hotel room

1   Listen to these key phrases.

Θέλω . . .	I want . . .
. . . ένα μονόκλινο	
. . . ένα δίκλινο	
. . . με μπάνιο	
. . . με ντους	

Βεβαίως!	Certainly!
Για πόσο καιρό;	How long for?
Για μία νύχτα / τρεις νύχτες	For one night / three nights

2   Listen to Mr Stakis asking for rooms. Does he want:

     a   two double rooms for two nights?
     β   a double and two singles for two nights?
     γ   a double and two singles for four nights?

3   Miss Petraki arrives at the hotel also looking for rooms, but the receptionist says: **Δυστυχώς, το ξενοδοχείο είναι γεμάτο** (Unfortunately, the hotel is full). She then asks: **Τι μπορώ να κάνω;** (What can I do?).

     a   Can you say what kind of room she is looking for?
     β   What alternative is suggested to her?

4   How would you say you want:

     a   on the first floor?   *γ*   for one night?

     β   for two nights?   *δ*   on the ground floor?

Booking ahead

1 Listen to these key phrases.

Μπορώ να κλείσω ένα δωμάτιο;	Can I book a room?
Για πότε;	When for?
Για σήμερα / αύριο	For today / tomorrow
Από την Τρίτη . . .	From Tuesday . . .
. . . μέχρι το Σάββατο	. . . until Saturday

Note that 'the' is used with the days of the week in Greek.

η Κυριακή (Sunday)	**η Πέμπτη** (Thursday)
η Δευτέρα (Monday)	**η Παρασκευή** (Friday)
η Τρίτη (Tuesday)	**το Σάββατο** (Saturday)
η Τετάρτη (Wednesday)	

2 Listen to a hotel receptionist taking bookings by phone. Can you fill in the missing information for each guest?

ΟΝΟΜΑ	από	μέχρι
ΣΟΦΟΥΛΗΣ	....	....
ΜΙΧΑΛΟΠΟΥΛΟΥ	....	....
ΘΩΜΟΓΛΟΥ	....	....
ΘΥΜΑΡΑΣ	....	....

What is the problem for Mr Thimaras?

Making requests

I Listen to these key phrases.

Μπορώ να ...   Can I ...
... έχω το κλειδί μου;   ... have my key?
... κάνω ένα τηλέφωνο;   ... make a telephone call?
... δω το δωμάτιο;   ... see the room?
... πληρώσω με κάρτα / Βίζα;   ... pay by (credit) card / Visa?

2 In the busy **Ξενοδοχείο Ζευς**, guests ask Athina if they can do or have something. Can you ascertain who asks what?

ο **Κύριος Δημητρίου**	make a telephone call
	book a room
η **Κυρία Αγγελοπούλου**	have their key
	see the room on offer
ο **Κύριος Βαννάς**	pay by Visa

στα Ελληνικά ...

in all the above requests, **μπορώ να** can be replaced by **θέλω να** to say that you 'want to' do something, e.g.
Θέλω να κάνω ένα τηλέφωνο (*I want to* make a telephone call).

3 Listen to the following exchanges and indicate with a **μπ** for **μπορώ** or a **θ** for **θέλω** in the space provided which word is used in each request. Then complete the requests by matching the Greek and English (phrases and illustrations). Listen out for the word **ψιλά**, meaning '(small) change'.

α .... **να έχω**   I

β .... **να κλείσω**   2   the taxi

γ .... **να δω**   3

δ .... **να πληρώσω**   4   my passport

Put it all together

1 Match the Greek with the English:

α Έχω κλείσει . . .   Certainly
β Δυστυχώς   I want to see . . .
γ Μπορώ να κλείσω . . . ;   Unfortunately
δ Βεβαίως   I've booked . . .
ε Θέλω να δω . . .   Can I book . . .?

2 Complete the dialogue below with words from the box. Note that **ή** written with an accent means 'or'.

Guest   **Καλημέρα. Θέλω να κλείσω ένα** .... (1) ....

Receptionist **Θέλετε** .... (2) .... **ή δίκλινο;**

Guest   **Ένα δίκλινο παρακαλώ.**
              Με .... (3) ....

Receptionist **Για** .... (4) .... **καιρό;**

Guest   **Από σήμερα μέχρι την**
              .... (5) ....

Receptionist **Βεβαίως. Δωμάτιο νούμερο 25**
              στον .... (6) ..... **όροφο.**
              Ορίστε το κλειδί σας.

> Τετάρτη
> μονόκλινο
> δωμάτιο
> πόσο
> πρώτο
> μπάνιο

3 Complete the following:

α Έχω κλείσει . . .
β Θέλω να πληρώσω με . . .
γ Μπορώ να κάνω . . .
δ Μπορώ να έχω . . .

Now you're talking!

1 Imagine you are Dimitra Kakouli, arriving at the **Ξενοδοχείο Μελίνα**. Prepare your part of the dialogue as indicated below, then practise with the audio.

◇ **Καλησπέρα σας. Ορίστε.**
◆ Greet the receptionist and say you have booked a room.
◇ **Το όνομά σας παρακαλώ;**
◆ Tell him your name.
◇ **Α ναι . . . ένα μονόκλινο με μπάνιο.**
◆ Say yes, for three nights.
◇ **Εντάξει. Το διαβατήριό σας παρακαλώ.**
◆ Say 'here you are' and ask where the room is.
◇ **Είναι στο δεύτερο όροφο. Νούμερο 31.**

2 This time you are Yannis Simis, arriving at the hotel with your wife and teenage son. Using the information depicted below, prepare to answer the receptionist's questions about your requirements. Start by asking if they have any rooms.

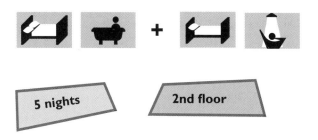

Quiz

1 How would you say you want a room 'for one night'?
2 If a hotel receptionist says **Το ξενοδοχείο είναι γεμάτο** what
   does he / she mean?
3 How do you say 'from Saturday until Wednesday'?
4 What are the Greek words for 'today' and 'tomorrow'?
5 How do you say 'What can I do?' in Greek?
6 What is 'or' in Greek?
7 Can you rearrange these words to form a sentence?
   ένα / κλείσω / ντους / να / με / Θέλω / δίκλινο
8 You want a room on the ground floor. How do you ask for it?

Now check whether you can . . .

■ say you have booked a room

■ ask for a room, specifying single or double and on what floor

■ say whether you want a room with bathroom or shower

■ say how long you want it for, from when and specify which days

■ ask for permission to do, or say you want to do something

■ respond to questions and requests by the hotel receptionist

As you work through this course and learn more about how the
Greek language works, go back over previous units, not just revising
but also applying your new knowledge to known words and phrases.
You will be surprised and encouraged to realise how much you
already know. You can increase that knowledge all the time. For
example, now you know how to form plurals, you can go back to
Unit 4 and practise ordering two beers – **δύο μπύρες παρακαλώ**.
Or, having learnt how to say 'my', etc. in Unit 3, you can work out
how to say 'my passport' – **το διαβατήριό μου**. Can you also work
out how to say 'Goodnight'? The answer's on page 113.

9 εννιά

Τι ώρα φεύγει;

- ● asking about public transport
- ● finding out travel times
- ● buying tickets
- ... and checking travel details

στην Ελλάδα και στην Κύπρο . . .

the most common form of public transport on land
is the bus (**το λεωφορείο**), and from island to island
the boat (**το καράβι**), or ferry (**το φέρρυ-μποτ**).
Ferry services are subject to seasonal and weather
variations, so check your journey details in advance.
Tickets are issued from a **ΠΡΑΚΤΟΡΕΙΟ** (ticket
agency), at the coach station, the harbour, and
sometimes on board. The greatly improved mainland
train network now links the major Greek towns and
can be a pleasant way of getting around.
However you decide to travel, you are sure to hear
'Have a good journey' – **Καλό ταξίδι!**

Asking about public transport

1 Listen to these key phrases.

(Κάθε πότε) έχει . . .   (How often) is there . . .
. . . καράβι για τη Σάμο;   . . . a boat for Samos?
. . . λεωφορείο για τα Μετέωρα;   . . . a bus for Meteora?
Έχει καράβι . . .   There's a boat . . .
. . . κάθε ώρα / μισή ώρα   . . . every hour / half hour
. . . κάθε πρωί / μέρα   . . . every morning / day

2 Martin, holidaying in a local resort, wants to visit the museum in Thessaloniki. Listen as he asks about transport and says: **Πού μπορώ να πάρω εισιτήριο;** (Where can I get a ticket?)

How often does the bus run and where can he buy a ticket?

στα Ελληνικά . . .

many place names, particularly those of the islands, are feminine, despite ending in **-ος**. So after **σε** (in/at/to), **για** (for), and **από** (from), the feminine word for 'the' is used, e.g. **στην Κύπρο, για τη Ρόδο, από την Τήνο.** Remember to omit the final **ς** from the place names.

3 Listen to some travel enquiries and fill in the information below.

By . . .	Where to?	When?
Αεροπλάνο (aeroplane)	....	....
Πούλμαν (coach)	....	....
Φέρρυ-μποτ (ferry)	....	....

4 How would you ask: 'How often is there a **Δελφίνι** ('Flying Dolphin' hydrofoil) for Paros / Mykonos / Lefkada?'

Finding out travel times

I Listen to these key phrases.

Τι ώρα φεύγει (το τραίνο);	What time does it (the train) leave?
Τι ώρα φτάνει (στην Ολυμπία);	What time does it arrive (at Olympia)?
Φεύγει σε μισή ώρα	It leaves in half an hour
Φτάνει σε δέκα λεπτά	It arrives in ten minutes
Πόση ώρα είναι το ταξίδι;	How long does the journey take?

στα Ελληνικά . . .

the day is divided into **το πρωί** the morning, **το μεσημέρι** midday to early afternoon, **το απόγευμα** late afternoon to early evening, **το βράδυ** later evening and **η νύχτα** the night.

---

2 Listen to three people enquiring about the departure and arrival times of trains to three Greek towns. Then note down the times, indicating a.m. (**π.μ.**) or p.m. (**μ.μ.**) and say how long the journey takes: **Το ταξίδι είναι . . . ώρες**.

	φεύγει στις	**φτάνει στις**	**ώρες**
α **Λάρισα**	....	....	....
β **Κόρινθος**	....	....	....
γ **Καβάλα**	....	....	....

3 At an information desk you overhear some people making enquiries about public transport to various places. Listen and decide whether the following statements are true or false.

		Ναι	**Όχι**
α	The bus for Glyfada leaves every 20 minutes.	■	■
β	The train from Lamia arrives at 5.30 p.m.	■	■
γ	The train to Athens leaves in one hour.	■	■

Buying tickets . . .

1 Listen to these key phrases.

Θέλω ένα εισιτήριο	I want a / one ticket
απλό / με επιστροφή	single / return
Θέλουμε δύο εισιτήρια . . .	We want two tickets . . .
. . . για αύριο το πρωί	. . . for tomorrow morning
. . . για σήμερα το βράδυ	. . . for this evening
. . . για την Παρασκευή το απόγευμα	. . . for Friday afternoon

στα Ελληνικά . . .

we have seen how verb endings change according to the person involved. Here we are using the 'we' and 'they' endings of the verb **θέλω** (I want): **θέλουμε** <u>we</u> want, **θέλουνε** <u>they</u> want.

Many Greek verbs follow the same pattern as **θέλω**, e.g. **κάνω** (to do), **φεύγω** (to leave), **μένω** (to live) and **δουλεύω** (to work).

However, there are some that do not: e.g. to go / I go (**πάω**), which is set out in full on page 121.

2 Listen to some people buying bus tickets at a **πρακτορείο**. First indicate in the grid how many tickets they buy and what kind they are, then note down the time of travel.

Destination	How many?	Single/Return	Time of travel
α Nafplio	....	....	....
β Tripoli	....	....	....
γ Volos	....	....	....
δ Preveza	....	....	....
ε Sparta	....	....	....

. . . and checking travel details

3 Listen to these key phrases.

Από πού φεύγει (το πούλμαν);   Where does it (the coach) leave from?

Αυτό είναι το καράβι για την Ύδρα;   Is this the boat for Hydra?

Πού πάει (αυτό το λεωφορείο);   Where does it (this bus) go?

4 Three travellers check their travel details at a **πρακτορείο**. Listen and then fill in the details of their itinerary.

	Destination **για πού;**	Leaving from **από πού;**
α	....	....
β	....	....
γ	....	....

στα Ελληνικά . . .

to say 'this' or 'that' with a noun you must also use the appropriate word for 'the', e.g.   **αυτός <u>ο</u> σάκος**   this/that holdall (m.)
                                αυτή <u>η</u> πτήση   this/that flight (f.)
                                αυτό <u>το</u> πούλμαν   this/that coach (n.)

5 Now practise asking: 'Where does this / that .... go to?' using the nouns: **το αεροπλάνο**, **το τραίνο**, and **το καράβι**.

6 Listen to the announcements at a Nicosia bus depot and match the bus numbers with the information on the screen. Listen for **έχει καθυστέρηση** which means 'is delayed'.

1	Arriving from Ayia Napa
6	Going to Paphos
20	Delayed, arriving in ½ hour
12	Leaving in ½ hour

Put it all together

1 After reading this train timetable decide whether the statements in Greek below are true or false. Then correct the false statements.

		1	2	3
Αθήνα	αν.	06.00	07.00	14.00
Λάρισα	αφ.	11.00	12.00	
	αν.	11.30	12.30	
Θεσσαλονίκη	αφ.		15.30	22.00
	αν.		15.45	
Ξάνθη	αφ.		19.45	
	αν.		19.50	
Αλεξανδρούπολη	αφ.	20.30	21.50	

αν. = departure
αφ. = arrival

α **Το πρώτο τραίνο φεύγει από την Αθήνα στις εφτά το πρωί.**

β **Το ταξίδι για τη Λάρισα είναι πέντε ώρες.**

γ **Το δεύτερο τραίνο φεύγει από την Ξάνθη στις οχτώ παρά δέκα.**

δ **Το τρίτο τραίνο φτάνει στη Θεσσαλονίκη στις δέκα το πρωί.**

ε **Το τρίτο τραίνο πάει στην Αλεξανδρούπολη.**

ζ **Το δεύτερο τραίνο δεν φτάνει στη Θεσσαλονίκη στις τρεις και μισή.**

2 Fill the gaps in the dialogue with the words from the box.

Καλημέρα. Έχει Δελφίνι .... **τη Σκιάθο αύριο;**

Ναι, ... **τέσσερα.**

.... **πότε φεύγουνε;**

Κάθε δύο .... **από τις οχτώ το** ....

Πού μπορώ .... **πάρω εισιτήριο;**

Από 'δω. Πόσα ....;

Ένα .... **για τις** .... **το μεσημέρι.**

Απλό;

Όχι, με ....

Κάθε		πρωί
	εισιτήριο	
επιστροφή		θέλετε
	δώδεκα	έχει
για	να	ώρες

Now you're talking

I Your island-hopping holiday is coming to a close and you need to get back to Athens for your return flight. First you ask a Greek friend about the ferries.

- ◆ Ask how often there is a ferry to Athens.
- ◇ **Έχει κάθε μέρα, το πρωί.**
- ◆ Ask what time it leaves.
- ◇ **Στις δέκα η ώρα.**
- ◆ Ask where you can get a ticket.
- ◇ **Στο πρακτορείο.**

2 The next day you go to get your ticket.

- ◆ Greet the clerk and say you want a single ticket for Athens.
- ◇ **Εντάξει. Για πότε είναι;**
- ◆ Say for today and ask where it leaves from.
- ◇ **Από το Ακρωτήρι.**

At Akrotiri you see two ferries.
- ◆ Ask a fellow traveller, 'Is that the ferry for Athens?'
- ◇ **Ναι, αυτό είναι.**

3 In Athens, another friend is taking you to the airport. On the way he asks you about your flight (**η πτήση**). You need to be able to say:

- ◆ your flight home leaves at 7 p.m.
- ◆ the flight arrives in London at 8.30
- ◆ you have a return ticket
- ◆ it costs £199 (**λίρες**).

Quiz

1 An airport announcement says: '**Η πτήση έχει καθυστέρηση**'. What do you understand?
2 If you wanted a return ticket would you ask for **ένα εισιτήριο απλό** or **ένα εισιτήριο με επιστροφή**?
3 If **φεύγω** means 'I leave', how would you say 'we leave'?
4 Is 'in two hours' **στις δύο η ώρα** or **σε δύο ώρες**?
5 How would you say, 'Where is this coach going?'?
6 Which word is missing in each of the following:
   Αυτή .... **πτήση / Αυτός** .... **σάκος / Αυτό** .... **τραίνο**?
7 What word is needed to make this phrase mean 'every ten minutes'?:
   .... **δέκα λεπτά**.
8 What word would you change to make the following mean 'the boat from Crete'?: **Το καράβι για την Κρήτη.**
9 How would you say 'this morning'?

Now check whether you can . . .

■ enquire about the availability of public transport

■ ask about departure and arrival details and understand the answer

■ find out where to buy tickets

■ buy a ticket and specify details

■ confirm which is the right bus, ferry, etc.

As you are nearing the end of this course, go back over all the *Now you're talking!* dialogues and practise them until you can say them fluently without using the *Audio script and answers*. Then you will have plenty of useful words and phrases at your fingertips for the next time you visit Greece or Cyprus.

Καλή όρεξη!

- asking what's on the menu
  - . . . and ordering food and drink
- expressing likes and dislikes
  - . . . and asking for more

στην Ελλάδα και στην Κύπρο . . .

a written menu does not always indicate what is available, and people often just ask the waiter what dishes are being served that day. You may be invited into the kitchen to look at the various dishes bubbling in pans and tureens to choose which ones look the most mouth-watering. The phrase **Τι είναι αυτό;** (What's this / that?) could come in useful here.

Greeks are great meat-eaters and vegetarian dishes are not widely available. However, if you ask **Τι έχετε για χορτοφάγους;** (What have you got for vegetarians?) you are sure to be offered a range of vegetable and salad dishes. So enjoy your meal – **Καλή όρεξη!**

Asking what's on the menu . . .

I Look at the menu below and see how much of it you can recognize or guess. Then check any unknown items in the glossary.

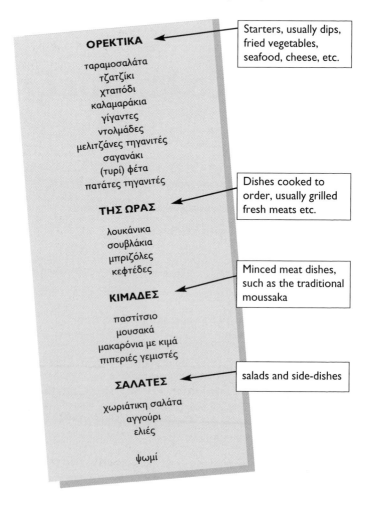

ΟΡΕΚΤΙΚΑ ← Starters, usually dips, fried vegetables, seafood, cheese, etc.

ταραμοσαλάτα
τζατζίκι
χταπόδι
καλαμαράκια
γίγαντες
ντολμάδες
μελιτζάνες τηγανιτές
σαγανάκι
(τυρί) φέτα
πατάτες τηγανιτές

ΤΗΣ ΩΡΑΣ ← Dishes cooked to order, usually grilled fresh meats etc.

λουκάνικα
σουβλάκια
μπριζόλες
κεφτέδες

ΚΙΜΑΔΕΣ ← Minced meat dishes, such as the traditional moussaka

παστίτσιο
μουσακά
μακαρόνια με κιμά
πιπεριές γεμιστές

ΣΑΛΑΤΕΣ ← salads and side-dishes

χωριάτικη σαλάτα
αγγούρι
ελιές

ψωμί

2 Listen to a waiter reciting what dishes are available, and tick the items you hear on the menu above.

. . . and ordering food and drink

3 Listen to these key phrases.

Τι έχετε σήμερα;	What have you got today?
Τι θα φάτε;	What will you have (eat)?
Θα πάρουμε. . .	We'll have . . .
. . . μία ντολμάδες	. . . one (portion of) stuffed vine leaves
. . . και μετά μία κεφτέδες	. . . and then one (portion of) meatballs

4 Listen to George ordering a meal for himself and his friend. Which of the dishes ordered is not on the menu opposite? Note in Greek you can simply use **μία** to order a portion of food (e.g. one meatballs).

5 Listen to these key phrases.

Τι θα πιείτε;	What will you drink?
Ένα μπουκάλι άσπρο κρασί	A bottle of white wine
Μισό κιλό κόκκινο κρασί	Half a kilo (litre) of red wine

6 Listen to Poppy and Christos ordering from the menu. Note that house wine, or wine from the barrel ('**βαρελίσιο κρασί**'), is ordered by the kilo, which is equivalent to a litre. For house wine, ask for **το δικό σας** (literally 'your own').

ΨΗΤΑ	ROAST MEATS	ΚΡΑΣΙΑ	WINES
αρνί	lamb	**κόκκινο**	red
χοιρινό	pork	**άσπρο**	white
μοσχάρι	veal	**ροζέ**	rosé
κοτόπουλο	chicken	**ρετσίνα**	retsina

- What kind of meat dish does Christos order?
- What two non-meat dishes are recommended for Poppy?
- What do they order to drink?

Expressing likes and dislikes

1 Listen to these key phrases.

Σας αρέσει η ρετσίνα;	Do you like retsina? (formal)
Σ'αρέσει η ρετσίνα;	Do you like retsina? (informal)
Μ'αρέσει ο μουσακάς	I like moussaka
Μ'αρέσουνε οι ελιές	I like olives
Δεν μ'αρέσουνε οι ελιές	I don't like olives

στα Ελληνικά . . .

when saying what you like and dislike, you use the appropriate word for 'the', placing it before the noun: **Μ'αρέσει <u>το</u> χταπόδι** (I like octopus), **Δεν σ'αρέσει <u>το</u> λάδι** (You don't like oil), **Σας αρέσουνε <u>τα</u> σουβλάκια;** (Do you like kebabs?). Refer to the grammar section on page 122 for an explanation of **μ'αρέσει**.

2 Practise saying whether you like or dislike the foods listed below using one of the expressions in the speech bubbles. Don't forget 'the'!

οι πιπεριές γεμιστές (1)
οι ντολμάδες (2)
η ταραμοσαλάτα (3)
το ψωμί (4)
το τζατζίκι (5)
οι πατάτες (6)
τα μακαρόνια με κιμά (7)

3 To say how much you like or dislike something, you can use the words **πολύ** (very much), and **καθόλου** (not at all). Listen to Fotis as he comments on some of the dishes above and write the number of the dish, as you hear it mentioned, in the appropriate box.

α Likes very much ▓▓▓   β Likes ▓▓▓

γ Doesn't like very much ▓▓▓   δ Doesn't like at all ▓▓▓

. . . and asking for more

4 Listen to these key phrases.

Μας φέρνετε . . .	(Could you) bring us . . .
. . . ακόμα ένα κιλό κρασί;	. . . another litre of wine?
. . . ακόμα λίγο ψωμί;	. . . some/a little more bread?
. . . το λογαριασμό;	. . . the bill?

στα Ελληνικά . . .

to ask for another or more of anything, use the word **ακόμα** + the
number or amount. e.g. **ακόμα ένα μπουκάλι κρασί**
ακόμα μία πατάτες
ακόμα δύο μπύρες
ακόμα λίγο τυρί

5 Fotis calls the waiter to the table. Listen out for **όλα εντάξει;**
– 'everything OK?'

- He asks the waiter for three more things. What are they?
- What dish does he especially like?

6 How would you order the following?

a another . . .

β another bottle of . . .

γ some more . . .

δ another portion of . . .

Put it all together

1 Match the Greek with the English.

a **Τι είναι αυτό;** | 1 What have you got today?
β **Μας φέρνετε . . . ;** | 2 We'll have . . .
γ **Το λογαριασμό παρακαλώ** | 3 Could you bring us . . . ?
δ **Και μετά . . .** | 4 What's this / that?
ε **Τι έχετε σήμερα;** | 5 And then . . .
ζ **Όλα εντάξει;** | 6 The bill, please
η **Θα πάρουμε . . .** | 7 Everything OK?

2 Number the following jumbled menu items 1, 2, 3 or 4 according to their correct headings.

ΟΡΕΚΤΙΚΑ (1)   **ΨΗΤΑ (2)**   **ΤΗΣ ΩΡΑΣ (3)**   **ΚΡΑΣΙΑ (4)**

χοιρινό		ντολμάδες		λουκάνικα		σουβλάκια	
κεφτέδες		μοσχάρι		κόκκινο		ροζέ	
αρνί		τζατζίκι		κοτόπουλο		ρετσίνα	
άσπρο		χταπόδι		καλαμαράκια		μπριζόλες	

3 In the following sentences add the correct endings to the verbs.

a **Μ'αρέσ____ οι μελιτζάνες τηγανιτές.**
β **Σας αρέσ____ το παστίτσιο;**
γ **Δεν μ'αρέσ____ τα λουκάνικα.**
δ **Μ'αρέσ____ πολύ το ούζο.**

4 Would you use **ακόμα ένα**, **ακόμα μία** or **ακόμα λίγο** with the following?

a .... **γίγαντες**
β .... **κρασί**
γ .... **μπουκάλι μπύρα**
δ .... **ψωμί**

Now you're talking!

Imagine you are on business in Greece and have invited your Greek colleague for a meal in a **ταβέρνα**. You can refer to the menu on page 88. The waiter greets you:

◊ **Καλησπέρα σας! Τι θα πιείτε;**
♦ Ask for a beer and half a litre of white wine.
◊ **Εντάξει.**

The waiter returns a few minutes later with the drinks.

◊ **Ορίστε. Τι θα φάτε;**
♦ Ask what he has today.
◊ **Έχουμε ορεκτικά, μπριζόλες, σουβλάκια, παστίτσιο και γεμιστά.**
♦ Order a portion of squid, taramosalata and a yogurt and cucumber dip.
◊ **Βεβαίως ... και μετά;**
♦ Ask your colleague if he likes macaroni pie.
◊ **Όχι πολύ. Θα πάρω μία ντομάτες γεμιστές.**
♦ Order two portions of stuffed tomatoes and a Greek salad.
◊ **Θέλετε πατάτες τηγανιτές;**
♦ Say no, we don't want chips.

The waiter brings the food.

◊ **Ορίστε. Καλή όρεξη!**
♦ Thank him for both of you and ask him to bring another beer.

Later the waiter returns and asks:

◊ **Θέλετε τίποτ' άλλο;**
♦ Say, no thank you, and ask for the bill.

Quiz

1 To say that you like **κεφτέδες** would you use **μ'αρέσει** or
 μ'αρέσουνε?
2 How do you say to the waiter 'Could you bring us the bill, please?'?
3 What dishes would be under the heading **ΤΗΣ ΩΡΑΣ**?
4 What two words would you add to **μ'αρέσει η φέτα** to mean
 'I *don't* like feta *at all*.'?
5 Can you name three types of meat in Greek?
6 How would you find out what's on the menu for vegetarians?
7 For 'another bottle of water', would you use **ακόμα ένα** or
 ακόμα μία?
8 If the waiter asks: **Τι θα φάτε;** what does he want to know?
9 How do you say 'Enjoy your meal!'?
10 When ordering a portion of anything, is the correct word to use
 ένα or **μία**?

Now check whether you can . . .

- ask and understand what's on the menu

- order a meal with drinks

- say what you like and don't like

- ask others what they like

Συγχαρητήρια! Congratulations! You have reached the end of
this course.

And now . . . prepare yourself for **Έλεγχος! 3** with some revision.
Listen to the conversations again – the more you listen, the more
confident you will become. You can test your knowledge of the key
phrases by covering up the English on the lists. Look back at the final
pages of each unit and use the quizzes and checklists to assess how
much you remember. Take every opportunity to speak Greek; if no
one else is available, talk out loud to yourself!

I You are an English business person arriving at the train station in Thessaloniki on a five-day business trip and need to get to your hotel quickly. Which of these questions would you ask?

α **Παρακαλώ, υπάρχει ξενοδοχείο εδώ κοντά;**

β **Συγνώμη, πού μπορώ να πάρω ταξί;**

γ **Συγνώμη, πού υπάρχει πρακτορείο;**

2 Having found a taxi you decide to check how much the fare will be. Listen and in reply to the driver's question **Πού πάτε;** (Where are you going?) say you're going to the Hotel Elektra. Then ask how much it is. For 'I go / I'm going' see Grammar, page 121.

Ταξιτζής	**Πού πάτε;**
Εσύ	....
Ταξιτζής	**Εντάξει.**
Εσύ	....
Ταξιτζής	**Δέκα ευρώ και πενήντα λεπτά.**

How much change would you get from a 20 euro note?

3 As you are driving along the taxi driver asks you about yourself. Listen carefully to the audio and reply to his questions.

4 You've already booked a single room with shower at the Hotel Elektra from today until Saturday. After giving your name at the hotel reception which of the following would you say?

α **Θέλω να κλείσω ένα μονόκλινο με ντους από σήμερα μέχρι το Σάββατο.**

β **Μήπως έχετε ένα δίκλινο με ντους μέχρι το Σάββατο;**

γ **Έχω κλείσει ένα μονόκλινο με ντους από σήμερα μέχρι το Σάββατο.**

δ **Έχω κλείσει ένα μονόκλινο με μπάνιο μέχρι το Σάββατο.**

5 Listen to the receptionist's reply. Make a note in English of the two things she asks you for. Then note your room number and which floor it's on.

α ....

β ....

γ **Δωμάτιο** .... **Όροφος** ....

6 The next stage of your trip requires you to visit Kavala for a week, so you ask the hotel receptionist for directions to the bus station ticket office. Listen and make a note of the directions she gives you.

Πού είναι το πρακτορείο;

....

7 At the bus station you ask how often there is a bus to Kavala, what time it leaves, and how much a return ticket costs. For each of the questions below choose the correct option.

α **Κάθε πότε / Τι ώρα** έχει λεωφορείο **από / για** την Καβάλα;

β **Τι ώρα φτάνει / φεύγει** από τη Θεσσαλονίκη;

γ **Πόσο κάνει / κάνουνε** ένα εισιτήριο **απλό / με επιστροφή;**

8 Now listen to the audio and make a note of the time the first bus leaves Thessaloniki and the time it arrives in Kavala. Then write down the price (**η τιμή**) of the ticket.

φεύγει	**φτάνει**	**τιμή**
....	....	....

9 In the hotel bar in Kavala, you meet Lefteris Apostolou, the Greek business contact who is accompanying you on your visits. He outlines your programme for the week. Listen and note down which days you are in the following places.

Ξάνθη   **Καβάλα**   **Δράμα**   **Θάσος**

10 Listen again and write down in English what Lefteris has planned for each day. **Ραντεβού** means 'appointment' or 'rendezvous'.

● (Monday)	(Thursday)
● (Tuesday)	(Friday)
● (Wednesday)	(Saturday)
●	(Sunday)

11 Having worked out your programme, you chat to Lefteris and ask him some questions about himself. His answers are below. Prepare your questions using the informal form, then be guided by the audio.

α ....
   Μένω εδώ στην Καβάλα με τη γυναίκα μου.

β ....
   Τη λένε Νάντια.

γ ....
   Ναι, έχω δύο παιδιά.

δ ....
   Είναι έξι και δέκα χρονών.

12 Now Lefteris asks you about yourself and offers you a drink. Listen to him on the audio and reply to his questions.

13 Read the poster advertising a restaurant and answer the questions below.

a What kind of restaurant is this?
β Name one house speciality.
γ Which word do you think means 'seafood'?
δ Is the restaurant closed tonight (Sunday)?
ε What kind of music would you expect to hear here?
ζ What kind of wines can you drink?
η Where is the restaurant located?

μπαλκόνι και ταράτσα

ελληνική μουσική

ΨΑΡΟΤΑΒΕΡΝΑ

ΤΑ ΤΡΙΑ ΚΑΛΑΜΑΡΙΑ

Πλατεία Αγ. Μαρίνας

Σπεσιαλιτέ : **Φρέσκα ψάρια και θαλασσινά (χταπόδι, καλαμαράκια) κτλ**

Ανοιχτά μέχρι 2.00 π.μ.

Κλειστά μόνο Δευτέρα

βαρελίσιο κρασί και ρετσίνα

κοντά στη θάλασσα

14 Look at the numbers and match the amounts to those on the bill.

a οχτώ ευρώ και ενενήντα λεπτά

β εκατόν δεκαέξι ευρώ

γ ένα και εβδομήντα πέντε

116

1,75

8,90

Audio scripts and answers

This section contains scripts of all the conversations. Answers that consist of words and phrases from the conversations are given in bold type. Other answers are given separately.

Unit 1 Καλημέρα!

Pages 8 & 9 Saying hello, goodbye and how are you?

2 • Γεια σας! (hello)
 • Καλημέρα σας! (good morning)
 • Γεια σου! (hello)
 • Καλημέρα! (good morning)
(Good morning: 2 + 4. Hello: 1 + 3)

3 • Γεια σου, Άννα!
 • Γεια σου, Πάνο!
 • Γεια σου, Στέλιο!
 • Γεια σου, Μαρία!
(Μαρία-4. Πάνο-2. Άννα-1. Στέλιο-3.)

5 • Γεια σας! Τι κάνετε;
 • Καλά, εσείς;
 • Πολύ καλά.

 • Καλημέρα σας! Τι κάνετε;
 • Καλά. Και εσείς, τι κάνετε;
 • Έτσι κ'έτσι.
(Τι κάνετε; *heard three times*)

6 • Καλημέρα σας!
 • Γεια σας! Τι κάνετε;
 • Καλά. Εσείς;
 • Πολύ καλά.

 • Καλημέρα!
 • Γεια σου! Τι κάνεις;
 • Καλά. Εσύ;
 • Πολύ καλά.
(The first is formal, the second informal)

7 1. α δ ε ζ θ   2. α δ ε ζ θ   3. β γ η θ

Pages 10 & 11 Saying what you're called and asking someone else's name

2 • Πώς σας λένε;
 • Με λένε **Αλέκο Καπετάνιο.**
 • Πώς σας λένε;
 • Με λένε **Μάνο Σαμαράκη.**
 • Πώς σας λένε;
 • Με λένε **Κατερίνα Παππά.**

3 • Καλημέρα, Γιάννη!
 • Γεια σου, Ιωάννα!
 • Γεια σου, Αλίκη!
 • Σπύρο, γειά!
1 Με λένε **Γιάννη.**   2 Με λένε **Ιωάννα.**
3 Με λένε **Αλίκη.**   4 Με λένε **Σπύρο.**

4 Με λένε + your name.

5 • Καλημέρα! Πώς σας **λένε;** (3)
 • **Με** (2) λένε Νίκο Σερετάκη.
 • Πώς **σας** (1) λένε;
 • Μαρία Παππά.
 • Γεια **σου!** (5) Πώς σε λένε;
 • Με λένε Αλίκη. Αλίκη Σαμαρά.
 • **Πώς** (4) σε λένε;
 • Σπύρο Σαμαρά.

6 • Πώς σας λένε;   (formal)
 • Με λένε Νίκο.
 • Νίκο. Πώς σε λένε;   (informal)
 • Με λένε Άννα.
 • Πώς σε λένε;   (informal)
 • Με λένε Γιάννη.
 • Πώς σας λένε;   (formal)
 • Με λένε Μαρία.

Page 12 Put it all together

1 Αα Εε Ιι Κκ Οο Ττ

2 ω-Ω Γ-γ η-Η Λ-λ μ-Μ Ν-ν
 Π-π ρ-Ρ Σ-σ/ς υ-Υ Ω-ω γ-Γ Υ-υ
 σ/ς-Σ Ρ-ρ π-Π ν-Ν Μ-μ λ-Λ Η-η

3 *1* yes *2* tee *3* lid *4* man *5* net
6 pull *7* red *8* sun *9* hot

Page 13 **Now you're talking!**

1 • **Καλησπέρα!**
• Καλησπέρα σας!
• **Με λένε Στέλιο Κάππα. Πώς σας λένε;**
• Με λένε Αντώνη Κορέλλη.

• **Πάνο! Κατερίνα! Γειά σας!**
• Γεια σου, Στέλιο! Τι κάνεις;
• **Πολύ καλά. (Και) εσείς;**
• Καλά, καλά!

• **Γειά σου, Αλίκη! Τι κάνεις;**
• Έτσι κ'έτσι.

2 • Καλημέρα σας!
• **Καλημέρα!**
• Πώς σας λένε;
• **Με λένε + your name.**
• Τι κάνετε;
• **Πολύ καλά.**
• **Και εσείς;**
• Αντίο!
• **Αντίο! / Γεια σας!**

Page 14 **Quiz**

1 **Γεια σας** or **Γεια σου**   *2* **σας**
3 **Γεια σου, Κώστα!**   *4* **Γεια σας!**
5 **Τι κάνετε;**   *6* It's the question mark
7 **Πώς σε λένε;**   *8* So-so
9 **Μ Ε Ι Α Κ Ν Τ Ο**
10 s   p   l   ee   o   g/y   n

Unit 2 Από πού είσαστε;

Pages 16 & 17 **Saying what nationality you are and where you're from**

• Καλημέρα, Κύριε Τζον. Είσαστε Άγγλος;
• Ναι, είμαι **Άγγλος**.
• Και εσείς, Κυρία Λίντα, είσαστε Αγγλίδα;

• Όχι. Είμαι **Σκωτσέζα**.
• Είσαστε Σκωτσέζος, Κύριε Πήτερ;
• Όχι. Είμαι **Αμερικανός**.
• Και εσείς, Κυρία Ανν;
• Είμαι **Ιρλανδέζα**.
John – English. Linda – Scottish.
Peter – American. Ann – Irish.

3 • Πάτση, είσαι **Αγγλίδα**;
• Ναι, είμαι!
• Εσύ, Πωλ, είσαι Άγγλος;
• Όχι. Είμαι **Σκωτσέζος**.
Patsy – English. Paul – Scottish.

5 **Από πού είσαστε;**
• Είμαι από την **Αγγλία**.
• Εσείς, από πού είσαστε;
• Από την **Αμερική**.
• Εσείς, είσαστε από την Αμερική;
• Όχι. Είμαι από την **Σκωτία**.
• Και εσείς;
• Είμαι από την **Ελλάδα**.
1 England – **Αγγλία**   *2* America – **Αμερική**   *3* Scotland – **Σκωτία**
4 Greece – **Ελλάδα**

6 • Εσύ, Ελένη, από πού είσαι;
• Δεν είμαι από την Ελλάδα. **Είμαι από την Κύπρο.**
• Α! Είσαι Κύπρια!
• Ναι. Εσύ;
• Είμαι Έλληνας – από την **Αθήνα**.
Eleni is from Cyprus. Haris is from Athens.

Page 18 **Saying if you're on holiday or business**

2 • Είσαστε εδώ για διακοπές;
• **Ναι.** Εσείς;
• **Όχι.** Είμαι εδώ για δουλειά.
woman – yes, man – no

3 • Γεια σας! Είσαστε ο Νίκος Σώτης;
• Όχι. Με λένε **Κώστα Λουκά**. Πώς σας λένε;
• Με λένε Kim Johnson. Είσαστε Έλληνας;
• Όχι. Είμαι **Κύπριος** – από τη **Λάρνακα**. Εσείς, από πού είσαστε;

- Είμαι από την **Αγγλία**.
- Είσαστε εδώ για διακοπές;
- **Όχι**. Εσείς;
- **Όχι**. Είμαι εδώ για δουλειά.

Man: *Costa Louka, Cypriot, from Larnaca, not on holiday. Woman: Kim Johnson, English, from England, not on holiday.*

Page 19 Using the numbers 0 to 12

2 5 2 10 12 7 9 3 11

3 Liverpool 4 Arsenal 0
Blackburn 2 Manchester United 1
Newcastle 5 Everton 6
Leeds 0 Chelsea 7
Wimbledon 12 Southampton 10

Page 20 Put it all together

2 taverna   theatre   dipsomania

3
Greece – Ελλάδα, Cyprus – Κύπρος,
England – Αγγλία, Scotland – Σκωτία,
Wales – Ουαλία, Ireland – Ιρλανδία
Australia – Αυστραλία, America – Αμερική.
Greek – Έλληνας, Cypriot – Κύπριος,
English – Άγγλος, Scottish – Σκωτσέζος,
Welsh – Ουαλός, Irish – Ιρλανδός,
Australian – Αυστραλός, American –
Αμερικανός.

Page 21 Now you're talking!

1
- **Γεια σας / Καλημέρα (σας).**
  Είσαστε Ελληνίδα;
- Ναι.
- **Από πού είσαστε;**
- Από την Αθήνα. Εσείς, από πού
  είσαστε;
- **Είμαι από την (Αγγλία).**
- Πώς σας λένε;
- **Με λένε . . .** (your name)

The woman is from Athens.

2
- Πώς σας λένε;
- **Με λένε Sam Collins.**
- Είσαστε Άγγλος;
- **Όχι, είμαι Αμερικανός.**
- Από πού είσαστε;
- **(Είμαι) από την Ατλάντα.**
- Είσαστε εδώ για δουλειά;
- **Ναι. (Είμαι εδώ για δουλειά.)**

3
- Καλημέρα!
- **Καλημέρα!**
- Τι κάνεις;
- **Καλά!**
- Από πού είσαι;
- **Είμαι από την (Αγγλία).**
- Είσαι εδώ για διακοπές;
- **Ναι. / Όχι. ([Δεν] είμαι . . .)**

Page 22 Quiz

1 **Είμαι από την Σκωτία** *2* **Είμαι
Έλληνας** *3* **μηδέν (0), δύο (2),
πέντε (5), εφτά (7), εννιά (9), δώδεκα
(12)** *4* **ένα (1), τρία (3), τέσσερα
(4), έξι (6), οχτώ (8), δέκα (10),
ένδεκα (11)** *5* **Είμαι εδώ για
διακοπές** *6* **Αγγλία** (It's a country –
the others are female nationals) *7* **Δεν**
είμαι από την Ουαλία *8* (Written) –
add Greek question mark: **;** (Spoken) –
rising intonation of the voice *9* **Από
πού είσαι;** *10* Max Peter Vera
Lawrence Katherine

Unit 3 **Αυτός είναι ο
Βαγγέλης**

Pages 24 & 25 Introducing friends and
family

2 Καλησπέρα Ελένη!
Καλησπέρα σας! Στέλλα – **αυτός** (2)
είναι ο (4) Μάικ, και **αυτή** (3) είναι η
(1) Παμ . . .

3 Mike, Pam – **αυτή είναι η Στέλλα.**

5 • Γεια σου, **Όλγα**! Τι κάνεις;
• Καλά, **Χρήστο**!
• Αυτός είναι ο άντρας σου;
• Ναι. Είναι ο **Δημήτρης**.
• Χαίρω πολύ. Αυτή είναι η γυναίκα μου, η **Σούλα**.
• Γεια σου!
Olga – Dimitris   Christos – Soula

6 • Αυτός είναι ο άντρας μου.
• Πώς **τον** λένε;
• **Τον** λένε Γιώργο.

Page 26 Saying how old you are

2 **τριάντα ένα, ογδόντα πέντε, είκοσι εννιά, εβδομήντα έξι, εξήντα τέσσερα, ενενήντα δύο**
Numbers not mentioned: 13 (**δεκατρία**), 21 (**είκοσι ένα**).

4 • Πόσο χρονών είσαστε, Κυρία Κούλα;
• Είμαι **είκοσι εννιά**. (**29**)

Page 27 Talking about family

2/3
• Εσείς, **Κυρία Άννα**, έχετε παιδιά;
• Ναι. έχω **ένα παιδί**.
• Και εσείς, **Κυρία Κούλα**;
• **Όχι. Δεν έχω παιδιά.**
• Εσείς, **Κύριε Τάκη**;
• Έχω **τέσσερα** παιδιά.
• Α! Πόσο χρονών είναι;
• Ο Πέτρος είναι **δεκαεννιά** (**19**) χρονών,
  Η Μαρίνα είναι **δώδεκα** (**12**),
  Η Έλλη είναι **εννιά** (**9**), και
  Ο Γιάννης είναι **εφτά** (**7**) χρονών.
2 Takis 4 children. Anna 1 child. Koula none;
3 See ages in brackets, above.

4 • Γιάννη, **έχεις** (2) παιδιά;
• Ναι, **έχω** (4) δύο.

• Παιδιά, πόσο χρονών **είσαστε**; (3)
• **Είμαι** (1) δέκα και ο Σάκης **είναι** (5) πέντε.

Page 28 Put it all together

2 (οικογένεια) eekoyeneea

3 Crewe; Wrexham; Perth; Limerick; Vancouver; Leicester; Wellington; Kilmarnock; Epsom; Phoenix.

4 *a* **Αυτή είναι η γυναίκα μου η Μαρία.**
  β **Έχω ένα παιδί, τον λένε Μανώλη.**
  γ **Πόσο χρονών είναι ο άντρας σου, Δώρα;**

Page 29 Now you're talking!

1 • **Καλημέρα (σας)!**
• Καλημέρα σας!
• **Είσαστε εδώ για διακοπές;**
• Ναι.
• **Πώς σας λένε;**
• Με λένε Θωμά.
• **Αυτή είναι η γυναίκα σας;**
• Ναι. Είναι η Αφροδίτη.
• **Χαίρω πολύ.**
• **Έχετε παιδιά;**
• Ναι. Δύο.
• **Πόσο χρονών είναι;**
• Είναι 12 και 16 χρονών.
• **Αυτός είναι ο άντρας μου, ο Σάϊμον.**
• Χαίρω πολύ!

2 • Είσαι εδώ για διακοπές;
• **Ναι. / Όχι. (Δεν) είμαι εδώ για διακοπές.**
• Από πού είσαι;
• **Είμαι από την + your country. / Είμαι + your nationality.**
• Πώς σε λένε;
• **Με λένε + your name.**
• Πόσο χρονών είσαι;
• **Είμαι (. . .) χρονών.**
• Έχεις παιδιά;
• **Ναι. Έχω (ένα παιδί / δύο παιδιά) etc. OR Όχι. Δεν έχω.**

Page 30 **Quiz**

1 **Αυτός είναι**   2 69   3 'Aftee eeneh ee feelee moo'   4 **Πώς τη λένε;**
5 'o' (Αυτός είναι **ο** Σταύρος.)
6 **Ο άντρας μου**   7 **είναι**   8 **είκοσι, σαράντα, εβδομήντα, εκατό(ν)**
9 **Έχω τρία παιδιά**

Unit 4 **Ένα καφέ παρακαλώ**

Pages 32 & 33 **Ordering a drink and a snack**

2 • – Ένα **καφέ** παρακαλώ. *(man 1)*
• – Μία **μπύρα**. *(woman 1)*
• – Μία **λεμονάδα** παρακαλώ. *(man 2)*
• – Ένα καφέ . . . όχι, ένα **τσάι**. *(woman 2)*

3 • Παρακαλώ;
• **Μία** ρετσίνα, **ένα** ούζο, **ένα** ουίσκυ, **μία** κοκακόλα, **ένα** Σπράϊτ και **μία** βότκα με τόνικ.

5 • Θέλω **ένα καφέ** και **ένα τοστ** με **τυρί** και **ζαμπόν** παρακαλώ.
• Καλά. Τι καφέ θέλετε;
• Ένα **Νεσκαφέ με γάλα**.
She orders a toasted sandwich with cheese and ham and an instant coffee with milk.

6 • Παρακαλώ;
• **Ένα τοστ** παρακαλώ. *(man 1)*
• Εντάξει. Εσείς;
• **Μία ομελέτα.** *(woman 1)*
• Και εσείς;
• **Ένα παγωτό.** *(man 2)*
• **Μία πάστα**, παρακαλώ. *(woman 2)*

7
α Ένα τσάι με γάλα και μία πάστα.
β Μία μπύρα και ένα τοστ με τυρί.
γ Μία ομελέτα με ζαμπόν και μία λεμονάδα.
δ Ένα παγωτό και ένα ελληνικό καφέ.

Page 34 **Offering someone a drink**

2 • Τι θα πάρεις, Άντα;
• Θα πάρω **ένα ουίσκυ** παρακαλώ.
• Με πάγο . . . νερό;
• **Με πάγο, χωρίς νερό.**
• Ορίστε.
• Ευχαριστώ πολύ.
She orders a whisky with ice – no water.

3 • Τι θα πάρεις Linda;
• **Μία σόδα παρακαλώ - με πάγο.** *(γ)*
• Εντάξει. Εσύ, John;
• **Ένα τζιν με τόνικ για μένα.** *(α)*
• Peter;
• **Θα πάρω ένα ούζο με νερό, παρακαλώ.** *(β)*
• Ορίστε.

4 α **Ένα Νεσ(καφέ) με γάλα παρακαλώ.**
β **Ένα ουίσκυ χωρίς πάγο παρακαλώ.**
γ **Ένα παγωτό παρακαλώ.**

Page 35 **Accepting or refusing a drink**

2 • Θα πάρετε ένα **ουίσκυ**;
• **Ναι**, ευχαριστώ – με πάγο.
• Θα πάρετε ένα **ούζο**;
• **Όχι**, ευχαριστώ.
• Θα πάρετε ένα **ελληνικό καφέ**;
• **Ναι**, ευχαριστώ - ένα γλυκό.
• Θα πάρετε **μία λεμονάδα**;
• **Όχι**, ευχαριστώ. Θα πάρω μία κοκακόλα.
Accepted: whisky, Greek coffee.
Refused: ouzo, lemonade.

3 • Θα πάρετε ένα ποτό, κυρία Χριστίνα;
• Όχι ευχαριστώ, Λάκη - θα πάρω ένα καφέ.
• Εσείς, κύριε Θανάση;
• Ναι, ευχαριστώ. Θα πάρω μία μπύρα.
• Ορίστε. Στην υγειά σας!
• Στην υγειά σου!

a **Ποτό** *usually refers to alcoholic drinks.*
β Lakis uses the formal version – **Στην**
υγειά σας *– Christina and Thanassis*
use the informal **Στην υγειά σου.**

Page 36 **Put it all together**

1 baklav**a** (a syrupy Greek pastry),
diskot**e**k (disco), gar**az** (garage),
kada**ee**fee (another sweet pastry).

2 **φ - καφέ, μ - ομελέτα, ν - ρετσίνα,
ζ - ούζο, λ -παρακαλώ, δ - σόδα,
ρ - μπύρα**

3 boutique   fast food   camping
discotheque   snack bar   breakfast
taverna   taxi

4 Καλησπέρα **σας**. Τι **θα** πάρετε;
Μία μπύρα για μένα, παρακαλώ.
Εντάξει. Και εσείς;
Ένα ούζο με πάγο.
Και **εσείς**, κύριε;
Θα **πάρω** ένα ελληνικό **καφέ και** ένα
κανταΐφι.

Page 37 **Now you're talking!**

1 • **Θα πάρετε ένα ποτό;**
• Ναι, ευχαριστώ! Ένα τζιν με τόνικ
  παρακαλώ.
• **Άρτα, τι θα πάρεις;**
• Μία μπύρα για μένα, παρακαλώ.
• **Εντάξει. Ένα τζιν με τόνικ, μία
  μπύρα – και ένα ουίσκυ (για
  μένα) παρακαλώ.**
• Με πάγο;
• Όχι ευχαριστώ.
  . . . **Ορίστε!**
• Ευχαριστούμε!
• **Στην υγειά σας!**
• Στην υγειά μας!

2 • Παρακαλώ;
• **Ένα τσάϊ με γάλα και ένα
  ελληνικό καφέ παρακαλώ.**
• Εντάξει. Θα πάρετε τοστ;
• **Ναι. Ένα τοστ με ζαμπόν και**

ένα (τοστ) με τυρί παρακαλώ.
• Ορίστε.
• **Ευχαριστούμε.**

3 • Θα πάρεις ένα ποτό;
• **Ναι, ευχαριστώ. Θα πάρω μία
  βότκα με λεμονάδα.**
• Με πάγο;
• **Όχι (χωρίς πάγο) ευχαριστώ.**
• Ορίστε.
• **Ευχαριστώ (πολύ). Στην υγειά
  σου!**

Page 38 **Quiz**
1 Με λεμόνι   2 **Ένα** καφέ – **ένα**
παγωτό – **μία** μπύρα – **μία** πάστα – **ένα**
τοστ – **ένα** ούζο – **μία** ομελέτα
3 'Please' and 'you're welcome'
4 **Στην υγειά σας!**
5 Panatheenaeekoss   6 **Εντάξει**
7 A syrupy Greek pastry   8 **ντ γκ μπ
αϊ**   9 **Ευχαριστούμε**   10 έχω

Έλεγχος! 1 (Pages 39–42)

1 • Καλημέρα σας! Πώς σας λένε;
• Με λένε **Σοφία** Dobson.
• Α! Είσαστε Αγγλίδα;
• Όχι. Είμαι **Ελληνίδα**. Ο άντρας μου
  είναι **Άγγλος**.
• Από πού είσαστε;
• Είμαι από την **Αθήνα**.
• Έχετε παιδιά;
• Ναι. Έχω ένα **αγόρι**.
• Πόσο χρονών είναι;
• Είναι **είκοσι. (20)**

2
a **ναι, ευχαριστώ!**
β **παρακαλώ**
γ **γεια σου!**
δ **έτσι κ'έτσι**
ε **χαίρω πολύ!**
ζ **στην υγειά σας!**
η **και εσύ;**
θ **εντάξει**

3 1 β   2 γ   3 δ   4 α

5 (1st column) **(Thes)salonika, Zakynthos/Zante, Aegina Nafplio(n);**
(2nd column) **Kefallonia, Halkidiki, Peloponnese, Corfu;**
(3rd column) **Nicosia, Limassol, Delphi, Olympia**

6 • **Πώς σας λένε;**
• Με λένε Ηρακλή Μαυρίδη.
• **Είσαστε εδώ για διακοπές;**
• Όχι, είμαι εδώ για δουλειά.
• **Από πού είσαστε;**
• Είμαι από την Κύπρο.
• **Πόσο χρονών είσαστε;**
• Είμαι 42 χρονών.
• **Έχετε παιδιά;**
• Ναι. Έχω δύο αγόρια και ένα κορίτσι.

7 Τον λένε **Ηρακλή** Μαυρίδη. Είναι εδώ για **δουλειά**. Είναι από την **Κύπρο**. Είναι **42** χρονών. Έχει τρία παιδιά – δύο **αγόρια** και ένα **κορίτσι**.

1 Πόσο χρονών είναι; – **Είναι σαράντα δύο χρονών.**
2 Είναι εδώ για δουλειά; – **Ναι. (Είναι εδώ για δουλειά).**
3 Έχει παιδιά; – **Ναι. Έχει τρία παιδιά. (Δύο αγόρια και ένα κορίτσι.)**
4 Πώς τον λένε; – **Τον λένε Ηρακλή Μαυρίδη.**
5 Από πού είναι; – **Είναι από την Κύπρο.**

8

Σ	Π	Ε	Ψ	Ο	Μ	Χ	Γ	Θ	Α	Ζ
Κ	Δ	Α	Ρ	Ε	Σ	Υ	Λ	Ι	Λ	Μ
Ε	Ε	Φ	Γ	Δ	Μ	Π	Υ	Ρ	Α	Ν
Τ	Α	Ο	Μ	Ω	Ρ	Δ	Κ	Λ	Ψ	Ο
Ο	Γ	Λ	Υ	Π	Τ	Α	Ο	Ε	Θ	Μ
Κ	Ζ	Ν	Χ	Ζ	Α	Ο	Σ	Μ	Τ	Π
Ο	Α	Ω	Ν	Κ	Ο	Α	Ν	Ο	Ξ	Α
Κ	Μ	Ε	Τ	Ρ	Ι	Ο	Ε	Ν	Ψ	Α
Ω	Π	Δ	Υ	Γ	Ν	Ε	Ρ	Α	Θ	Υ
Ξ	Ο	Ψ	Ρ	Ι	Α	Χ	Λ	Δ	Ζ	Η
Τ	Ν	Ε	Ι	Κ	Β	Τ	Γ	Α	Λ	Α

9
α **Γεια σου!**
β **Πώς σε λένε;**
γ **Από πού είσαι;**
δ **Αυτός είναι ο άντρας σου;**
ε **Έχεις παιδιά;**
ζ **Τι κάνεις;**

10 *a* €6.   *β* €2,20.   *γ* €1,60.
δ €1,50.   *ε* €1,40.   *ζ* €1,20.
η €4,60.   *θ* €2,50.

11 • Γεια σας. Τι θα πάρετε;
• Γεια σας. **Ένα τσάι, μία μπύρα, μία κοκακόλα και ένα ούζο με πάγο . . .**
• Εντάξει. Άλλο;
• Ναι. **Μία ομελέτα, ένα τοστ με τυρί, ένα σάντουϊτς με ζαμπόν και ένα παγωτό.**
• Bill comes to: € **2,10** + € **2,80** + € **1,50** + € **2** + € **4** + € **1,60** + € **1,60** + € **3,60** = € **19,20**

Unit 5 Υπάρχει τράπεζα εδώ;

Pages 44 & 45 **Asking what facilities are available and how to find them**

2 *a* - supermarket   *β* - chemist's
γ - toilet   *δ* - museum   *ε* - telephone
ζ - church

3 • Συγνώμη, υπάρχει **τηλέφωνο** εδώ;
• **Όχι**, συγνώμη.
• Υπάρχει **φαρμακείο** εδώ;
• **Ναι**, υπάρχει.
• Υπάρχει **μουσείο** εδώ;
• **Όχι**, δεν υπάρχει.
• Συγνώμη, υπάρχει **εκκλησία** εδώ;
• **Ναι**, είναι εκεί.
α **Όχι**   *β* **Ναι**   *γ* **Όχι**   *δ* **Ναι**

5 η τράπεζα   το περίπτερο
το ξενοδοχείο   το τηλέφωνο
το φαρμακείο   η τουαλέτα
η εκκλησία   το μουσείο

6 Συγνώμη, πού είναι το
σουπερμάρκετ;
Θα πάτε ίσια, θα στρίψετε δεξιά και
μετά **θα στρίψετε αριστερά.**
Ευχαριστώ πολύ.
She wants to go to the supermarket.
Go straight on.   Turn left.

Pages 46 & 47 **Understanding basic
directions and asking for help to
understand**

2 • Συγνώμη, υπάρχει ξενοδοχείο εδώ;
• Ναι. Είναι εκεί, **ίσια.**
• Υπάρχει τράπεζα εδώ;
• Ναι. Είναι **δεξιά.**
• Υπάρχει φαρμακείο εδώ;
• Ναι, **εδώ αριστερά.**
1 Chemist's   *2* Hotel   *3* Bank

3 • Υπάρχει **τράπεζα** εδώ;
• Ναι, υπάρχει.
• Είναι μακριά;
• Όχι, **είναι κοντά.** Μόνο 50 **μέτρα
από 'δω.**
To the bank.   It's near.   50 metres away.

**4 Πού είναι: το ταχυδρομείο;
ο φούρνος;
η τουαλέτα;**

6 Υπάρχει **ταχυδρομείο** εδώ κοντά;
Όχι, το **ταχυδρομείο είναι μακριά,**
υπάρχει μόνο **περίπτερο.**
Πού είναι το περίπτερο;
**Θα πάτε ίσια, θα στρίψετε δεξιά,
θα πάτε ξανά δεξιά και το
περίπτερο είναι εκεί, αριστερά.**
Συγνώμη, δεν κατάλαβα. **Το λέτε πιο
αργά, παρακαλώ;**
Α συγνώμη . . . (repeats above)
Ευχαριστώ πολύ.
Παρακαλώ.
Answers: a To the post office.   *β* There
isn't one nearby.   *γ* The kiosk.   *δ* To
speak more slowly.   *ε* No. 3 is the kiosk.

7 Συγνώμη, πού είναι το Θέατρο
Παλλάς;

(1) Θα πάτε ίσια, και μετά θα
στρίψετε δεξιά. Το θέατρο είναι
στα αριστερά σας.
**(2) Θα στρίψετε αριστερά εδώ και
το θέατρο είναι αριστερά.**
(3) Θα στρίψετε αριστερά, θα πάτε
ίσια και το θέατρο είναι δεξιά.
The second person gives the correct directions.

Page 48 **Put it all together**

2 *a* Is it near?   *β* It's on the right.
γ Turn left.   *δ* It's near here.
ε It isn't far.   *ζ* Don't go left.
η Go straight on.

3 η θάλασσα   η κλινική
το νοσοκομείο   ο σταθμός
το μοναστήρι   η παραλία
το γκαράζ   **το** εστιατόριο

Page 49 **Now you're talking!**

1 • **Γεια σας, υπάρχει εστιατόριο
εδώ κοντά;**
• Ναι. Το Εστιατόριο Άργος.
• **Είναι μακριά;**
• Όχι. Μόνο 50 μέτρα. Θα στρίψετε
δεξιά και μετά ξανά δεξιά.
• **Το λέτε ξανά παρακαλώ;**
• (Repeat above)
• **Ευχαριστώ πολύ. Πού είναι το
ασανσέρ;**
• Είναι εκεί, αριστερά.

2 • **Παρακαλώ! Υπάρχει τηλέφωνο;**
• Όχι, δεν υπάρχει τηλέφωνο. Θα
πάτε στο περίπτερο.
• **Δεν κατάλαβα. Το λέτε πιο
αργά παρακαλώ;**
• Υπάρχει τηλέφωνο στο περίπτερο.
• **Ευχαριστώ, πού είναι η
τουαλέτα;**
• Εδώ, αριστερά.

3 • **Πού είναι το νοσοκομείο;**
• Θα πάτε ίσια και θα στρίψετε δεξιά.
• **Πού είναι το γκαράζ;**
• Θα στρίψετε δεξιά και μετά
αριστερά.

- **Πού είναι ο σταθμός;**
- Θα πάτε ίσια.
- **Πού είναι η παραλία;**
- Θα στρίψετε αριστερά εκεί.

hospital: straight on, turn right; garage: turn right, then left; station: straight on; seafront: turn left.

Page 50 **Quiz**

1 **Υπάρχει σουπερμάρκετ / εστιατόριο / περίπτερο / γκαράζ εδώ;**   *2* **κοντά**
3 **Είναι μακριά;**   *4* ο / το / η   *5* right
6 **στο** περίπτερο   *7* **μετά**
8 **Το λέτε ξανά, παρακαλώ;**   *9* **Πού είναι: το μουσείο / η εκκλησία / το Ξενοδοχείο Ωμέγα / το τουριστικό γραφείο;**   *10* Omit **δεν :   Κατάλαβα!**

Unit 6 **Πού μένετε;**

Pages 52 & 53 **Talking about where you live and work**

2 • Πού μένεις, Θανάση;
• Μένω εδώ **στο** Ναύπλιο, αλλά είμαι από **την** Άγια Νάπα **στην** Κύπρο.

3
Oxford	Madrid
Edinburgh	New York
Melbourne	Berlin
Dublin	Paris

a Ο Simon μένει στην Οξφόρδη, και η Carmen είναι από τη Μαδρίτη.
β Η Maureen μένει στο Εδιμβούργο, και ο Burt είναι από τη Νέα Υόρκη.
γ Η Kylie μένει στη Μελβούρνη, και ο Fritz είναι από το Βερολίνο.
δ Ο Patrick μένει στο Δουβλίνο, και η Monique είναι από το Παρίσι.

5 • Πού δουλεύεις, **Κική**;
• Δουλεύω για τη **SONY.**
• Εσύ, **Παύλο**, πού δουλεύεις;
• Δουλεύω **σε** σχολείο.
• Και εσύ, **Λούλα**;
• Εγώ δουλεύω **σε νοσοκομείο**.

School - Pavlos. Hospital - Loula. SONY - Kiki.

6 • Γεια σου, Αντώνη! Πού δουλεύεις τώρα;
• **Δουλεύω στη Λάρισα, και μένω εκεί.**
• Ναι; Και η γυναίκα σου δουλεύει εκεί;
• **Όχι. Αυτή δεν δουλεύει τώρα.**

a Antonis   β Antonis' wife   γ Larissa

Page 54 **Getting more directions**

2 • Συγνώμη, πού είναι το Ξενοδοχείο Όλγα;
• Είναι **απέναντι από** το μουσείο.
• Πού είναι η εκκλησία;
• **Κοντά στην** πλατεία.
• Συγνώμη, πού είναι το φαρμακείο;
• Το φαρμακείο είναι **δίπλα στο** σινεμά.

a opposite   β near   γ next to

3
a Υπάρχει εστιατόριο **κοντά στην παραλία**.
β Η τράπεζα είναι **απέναντι από το ξενοδοχείο**.
γ Υπάρχει φαρμακείο **δίπλα στο νοσοκομείο**.
δ Το μουσείο είναι **μακριά από το λιμάνι**.

Page 55 **Finding out about opening hours**

2
a Τι ώρα ανοίγει το μαγαζί;
Το μαγαζί ανοίγει στις οχτώ η ώρα και κλείνει στις εφτά.
β Και το εστιατόριο;
Το εστιατόριο ανοίγει στις δώδεκα και κλείνει στις ένδεκα και μιση.
γ Και το γκαράζ;
Το γκαράζ ανοίγει στις εφτά η ώρα και κλείνει στις τέσσερις.
*a 8.00–7.00   β 12.00–11.30
γ 7.00–4.00*

3 Τι ώρα είναι;
1 Είναι **εννιά παρά τέταρτο.** (8.45)
Τι ώρα είναι;
2 Είναι **ένδεκα και μισή.** (11.30)
Τι ώρα είναι;
3 Είναι **οχτώ και τέταρτο.** (8.15)
Τι ώρα είναι;
4 Είναι **εφτά η ώρα.** (7.00)
Τι ώρα είναι;
5 Είναι **μία παρά τέταρτο.** (12.45)

4
α Είναι **τρεις παρά τέταρτο.**
β Είναι **τέσσερις και μισή.**
γ Είναι **μία και τέταρτο.**

Page 56 Put it all together

1 α I work; *β* she is; *γ* you do
(formal); *δ* you live (informal);
ε he has; *ζ* it opens

2 α **σε** *β* **στην** *γ* **για τη**
    δ **από το** *ε* **από την**

3
α **Η τράπεζα ανοίγει στις εννιά και
μισή και κλείνει στις τέσσερις και
μισή.**
β **Το φαρμακείο ανοίγει στις οχτώ
(η ώρα) και κλείνει στις έξι (η
ώρα).**
γ **Το τουριστικό γραφείο ανοίγει
στις δέκα (η ώρα) και κλείνει στις
πέντε και μισή.**
δ **Το εστιατόριο ανοίγει στις εφτά
(η ώρα) και κλείνει στις
δώδεκα και μισή.**

Page 57 Now you're talking!

1 • **Γειά σου, Δάφνη. Με λένε Susan
Lord.**
• Καλημέρα, Σούζαν. Μένεις εδώ;
• **Ναι. Μένω εδώ στο York.**
• Πού δουλεύεις;
• **Δουλεύω σε τουριστικό γραφείο
στο Ληντς.**
• Το Ληντς είναι μακριά από 'δω;
• **Όχι. Είναι πολύ κοντά.**

2 • Πού είναι η τράπεζα;
• **Η τράπεζα είναι δίπλα στο
Σινεμά Ριτζ, απέναντι από την
εκκλησία.**
• Τι ώρα ανοίγει;
• **Ανοίγει στις εννιά και μισή και
κλείνει στις πέντε η ώρα.**

3 • **Πού μένεις;**
• Μένω στη Βέροια.
• **Είναι κοντά στην Αθήνα;**
• Όχι, είναι κοντά στη Θεσσαλονίκη.
• **Δουλεύεις στη Βέροια;**
• Ναι, έχω μαγαζί εκεί.

4 • Πού μένετε;
• **Μένω στο +** *name of place.*
• Είναι κοντά στο Λονδίνο;
• **Ναι / Όχι. (Είναι κοντά στο /
μακριά από το Λονδίνο)**
• Μένετε στο κέντρο;
• **Ναι / Όχι, (δεν) μένω στο
κέντρο.**
• Δουλεύετε;
• **Ναι, δουλεύω σε +** *place of work*
/ για την + *name of company.* OR
Όχι, δεν δουλεύω.

Page 58 Quiz

1 **Πού μένετε;** *2* **σε γραφείο**
3 **ταχυδρομείο** (post office),
φαρμακείο (chemist's), **εστιατόριο**
(restaurant). *4* **απέναντι από το**
5 **στο** Λονδίνο, **στην** Κρήτη, **στη** Νέα
Υόρκη *6* Το μαγαζί κλείνει **στις** δέκα η
ώρα
7 **Δουλεύω για τη** Ford *8* Ο φίλος
μου **δουλεύει** μακριά από 'δω.

Unit 7 **Πόσο κάνει;**

**Page 60 Asking for something in a
shop**

2 Εντάξει. Θέλω . . . βούτυρο, τσιγάρα, ασπιρίνες, μπισκότα, γραμματόσημα, μαρμελάδα, γιαούρτι και ντομάτες.

He's forgotten grapes and cards.

3
εφημερίδες	βιβλία
ελιές	σάκοι
καρπούζια	τηλεκάρτες
μήλα	πορτοκάλια

Page 61 Saying how much you want

2
- Καλημέρα!
- Ορίστε, τι θέλετε;
- **Θέλω δύο κιλά μήλα, ένα κιλό σταφύλια, ένα καρπούζι και ένα τέταρτο ελιές . . . α ναι, και λεμόνια!**
- Πόσα λεμόνια θέλετε;
- **Μισό κιλό παρακαλώ.**
- Εντάξει. Θέλετε τίποτ' άλλο;
- Ναι. Μήπως έχετε φέτα και βούτυρο;
- Ναι. Πόσο θέλετε;
- **Μισό κιλό φέτα και ένα τέταρτο βούτυρο παρακαλώ.**

apples: 2 kilos; grapes: 1 kilo; water melons: 1;
olives: a quarter; lemons: half a kilo;
feta cheese: half a kilo; butter: a quarter.

3
- Γειά σας. **Μήπως έχετε γραμματόσημα;**
- Ναι, έχουμε. Πόσα θέλετε;
- **Θέλω τέσσερα - και τέσσερις κάρτες.**
- Ορίστε. Τίποτ' άλλο;
- Ναι . . . και **μία εφημερίδα παρακαλώ.**

Kiriakos wants 4 cards, 4 stamps and 1 newspaper.
(Ways of asking – see phrases underlined.)

4 Θέλω . . .
    ένα τέταρτο φέτα
    τρεις μπύρες
    τέσσερα γιαούρτια
    μισό κιλό βούτυρο
    μία τηλεκάρτα

Page 62 Asking the price of something

2
- Ορίστε, τι θέλετε;
- Θέλω ένα **μπουκάλι νερό** και ένα **φιλμ** παρακαλώ.
- Ορίστε το νερό. Δυστυχώς δεν έχουμε φιλμ.
- Καλά. Πόσο κάνει το **καπέλο**;
- Οχτώ λίρες.
- Και το **αντηλιακό**;
- Πέντε λίρες.
- Εντάξει. Και πόσο κάνουνε αυτά;
- Οι **σαγιονάρες**; Κάνουνε τρεις λίρες.

She asks the price of the hat, the sun-tan lotion and the flip-flops. Not mentioned – the beach umbrella.

3 Πόσο κάνουνε αυτά; *(plates + holdalls)*
Πόσο κάνει αυτό; *(picture or icon + set of worry beads)*
Πόσο κάνουνε **τα πιάτα**; *(plates)*
Πόσο κάνει **η εικόνα**; *(picture or icon)*
Πόσο κάνουνε **οι σάκοι**; *(holdalls)*
Πόσο κάνει **το κομπολόϊ**; *(set of worry beads)*

Page 63 Understanding amounts

2 Εντάξει . . .
    η τηλεκάρτα – **Τρία ευρώ,**
    τα τσιγάρα – **Δύο και εβδομήντα,**
    το τσάι – **Ένα ευρώ και εξήντα εννιά λεπτά,**
    οι ασπιρίνες – **Σαράντα πέντε λεπτά,**
    τα φιλμ – **Πέντε και εξήντα,**
    οι σοκολάτες – **Ένα ευρώ,**
    το Νεσκαφέ – **Έξι και είκοσι πέντε,**
    οι μπύρες – **Τρία και ογδόντα,**
    όλα μαζί – **Είκοσι τέσσερα ευρώ και σαράντα εννιά λεπτά.**

1 – €3 2 – €2,70 3 – €1,69 4 – €0,45
5 – €5,60 6 – €1 7 – €6,25 8 – €3,80
Altogether – €24,49

4 • Καλημέρα, τι θέλετε;
• **Πόσο κάνει ένα γραμματόσημο**
  για την Αγγλία;
• Εξήντα πέντε λεπτά.
• **θέλω δέκα (10) παρακαλώ.**
• Ορίστε. Τίποτ' άλλο;
• **Όχι, αυτά.**
• Έξι και πενήντα παρακαλώ

Page 64 **Put it all together**

1 1 δ   2 ε   3 α   4 β   5 γ

2 32,00 +
    8,50 +
    1,75
   ─────
   € 42,25
Change from € 50 note = € 7,75
(εφτά ευρώ και εβδομήντα πέντε
λεπτά)

3 (Μήπως) έχετε / θέλω: ψωμί /
πορτοκάλια / τυρί / ντομάτες / ζαμπόν /
ένα μπουκάλι νερό / ελιές / μπισκότα /
σταφύλια / σοκολάτες.

Page 65 **Now you're talking!**

1 • Καλημέρα. Τι θέλετε;
• **(Θέλω) ένα καρπούζι και ένα**
  κιλό μήλα παρακαλώ.
• Ορίστε, τίποτ' άλλο;
• **(Μήπως) έχετε ελιές;**
• Δυστυχώς, δεν έχουμε.
• **Εντάξει.**

2 • **Πόσο κάνει το βούτυρο;**
• Κάνει πέντε και εξήντα.
• **(Θέλω) μισό κιλό, και έξι**
  γιαούρτια παρακαλώ.
• Θέλετε τίποτ' άλλο;
• **Ναι. Θέλω ένα μπουκάλι γάλα**
  και μία μαρμελάδα, παρακαλώ.
• Ορίστε. Αυτά;
• **Ναι, αυτά. Πόσο κάνουνε όλα**
  μαζί;

3 • Ορίστε παρακαλώ.
• **Μήπως έχετε ασπιρίνες;**
• Ναι. Ορίστε. Τίποτ' άλλο;
• **Πόσο κάνει ένα γραμματόσημο**
  για την Ιρλανδία;
• 65 λεπτά.
• **Θέλω τρία γραμματόσημα για**
  την Ιρλανδία και ένα για την
  Αμερική παρακαλώ.

Page 66 **Quiz**

1 **Πόσο κάνουνε τα λεμόνια;**
2 **Τρία** κιλά ντομάτες   3 € 122,96
4 The lira, or pound (£)
5 **(Μήπως) έχετε τσιγάρα;**
6 Πόσο κάνει αυτό;   7 **Πόσο καφέ**
θέλετε;   8 ένα λεπτό.
9 **οι κάρτες – τα μπισκότα – τα φιλμ**
– τα καρπούζια   10 Ένα
γραμματόσημο για την Ελλάδα,
παρακαλώ.

Έλεγχος! 2 (Pages 67–70)

1
α **ΠΕΡΙΠΤΕΡΟ**
β **ΤΡΑΠΕΖΑ**
γ **ΚΑΦΕΤΕΡΙΑ**
δ **ΦΑΡΜΑΚΕΙΟ**
ε **ΣΟΥΠΕΡΜΑΡΚΕΤ**
ζ **ΤΑΧΥΔΡΟΜΕΙΟ**

2
α Το μουσείο είναι **στην πλατεία.**
   Ανοίγει στις **δέκα** και κλείνει στις
   τέσσερις και μισή.
   The museum is **in** the square.

β Το μοναστήρι του Αγίου Γεωργίου
   είναι **δίπλα στην εκκλησία, εκατόν**
   πενήντα μέτρα από 'δω.
   St George's monastery is **150** metres away.

γ Για το τουριστικό γραφείο **θα πάτε**
   ίσια και θα στρίψετε αριστερά στο
   σινεμά. Είναι εκεί, δεξιά.
   Turn **left** at the cinema. It's on the **right**.

3 ι - γ   2 - ζ   3 - δ   4 - θ   5 - η   6 - ε
    7 - β   8 - α

4

α   Η τράπεζα είναι αριστερά από το
    ξενοδοχείο.

β   Θέλω μισό κιλό τυρί και ένα
    καρπούζι, παρακαλώ.

γ   Το θέατρο είναι εκατό μέτρα από
    εδώ.

5   α **Το λέτε ξανά παρακαλώ;** (1)
    β **Πού είναι το τηλέφωνο;** (6)
    γ **Συγνώμη!** (3)
    δ **Πιο αργά παρακαλώ.** (2)
    ε **Δεν κατάλαβα.** (4)
    ζ **Υπάρχει τουαλέτα;** (5)

6

```
        Ε Δ Ω
  Θ Ε Λ Ω
        Δ Ο Υ Λ Ε Υ Ω
  Κ Λ Ε Ι Ν Ε Ι
  Ε Κ Κ Λ Η Σ Ι Α
  Τ Ε Τ Α Ρ Τ Ο
  Α Π Ε Ν Α Ν Τ Ι
    Ε Φ Η Μ Ε Ρ Ι Δ Α
Ν Υ Χ Τ Ε Σ
        Α Θ Η Ν Α
```

(Shaded word): **ΔΩΔΕΚΑΝΗΣΑ,** the
Dodecanese, meaning 12 islands

7   • Πόσο κάνει το ψωμί;
    • **50** λεπτά.
    • Πόσο κάνουνε **έξι** γιαούρτια;
    • **6** ευρώ και **96** λεπτά.
    • Πόσο κάνει ένα τέταρτο βούτυρο;
    • **3** και **5**.
    • Πόσο κάνουνε **πέντε** μπουκάλια
     κρασί;
    • **30** ευρώ.
    • Πόσο κάνει **μισό κιλό** καφέ;
    • **2** και **20**.
    • Πόσο κάνει **μία** σοκολάτα;
    • **65** λεπτά.

1 (loaf of) bread, € 0,50; 6 yoghurts, € 6,96;
¼ kilo butter, € 3,05; 5 bottles wine, € 30;
½ kilo coffee, € 2,20; 1 (bar of) chocolate,
€ 0,65.

8   *Total amount: β (€ 43,36)*

9   1 **Πού μένετε;**
    2 **Μήπως έχετε μπισκότα;**
    3 **Πόσο κάνουνε τα μήλα;**
    4 **Τι ώρα κλείνει η τράπεζα;**
    5 **Πόσο τυρί θέλετε;**
    6 **Θέλετε τίποτ' άλλο;**
    7 **Πού είναι το Εστιατόριο**
     Αλέξανδρος;
    8 **Δουλεύετε στην Ελλάδα;**
    α - 6   β - 3   γ - 8   δ - 4   ε - 2   ζ - 5
    η - 1   θ - 7

10 α **Ναι,**   β **Όχι** (He lives **near** Lamia),
    γ **Ναι,**   δ **Όχι** (He's 40),   ε **Ναι**

11 Με   Είμαι   είμαι   Δουλεύω
    μένω   Έχω   μου

Unit 8 Θέλω ένα δωμάτιο

Page 72 **Checking in at reception**

2   • Καλησπέρα. Έχω κλείσει **ένα**
     δωμάτιο.
    • Το όνομά σας, παρακαλώ.
    • **Μακρή Σοφία.**
    • Α ναι, στον **πρώτο όροφο.**
     Δωμάτιο 26. Το κλειδί σας, κυρία
     Μακρή.

    • Γεία σας. Έχω κλείσει **ένα δωμάτιο**
     στο όνομα **Παυλίδης – στο**
     ισόγειο.
    • Ναι. Δωμάτιο **11. Το διαβατήριό**
     σας, παρακαλώ.

    • Γεία σας. Έχω κλείσει **δύο δωμάτια.**
     Το όνομά μου είναι **Ιωαννίδης**
     Στέφανος.
    • Εντάξει. **35 και 37, στο δεύτερο**
     όροφο. Ορίστε τα κλειδιά σας.

Κος. Παυλίδης	1,	11,	ground
Σ. Μακρή	1,	26,	1st
Σ. Ιωαννίδης	2,	35 + 37,	2nd

3   *Mr. Pavlides is the Cypriot.*

Page 73 **Finding a hotel room**

2 • Μήπως έχετε δωμάτια;
• Βεβαίως! Τι δωμάτια θέλετε;
• **Θέλω ένα δίκλινο και δύο μονόκλινα.**
• Για πόσο καιρό είναι;
• **Για δύο νύχτες.**
β *He wants a double and two singles for two nights.*

3 • Καλημέρα. Θέλω **ένα μονόκλινο με ντους,** παρακαλώ.
• Δυστυχώς το ξενοδοχείο είναι γεμάτο.
• Αχ . . . τι μπορώ να κάνω;
• **Θα πάτε στο Ξενοδοχείο Μεταξά, απέναντι.**
α *She wants a single with shower.*
β *She is told to go to the Hotel Metaxa opposite.*

4
α **ένα μονόκλινο στον πρώτο όροφο**
β **ένα δίκλινο με μπάνιο για δύο νύχτες**
γ **δύο δίκλινα για μία νύχτα**
δ **ένα μονόκλινο με ντους στο ισόγειο**

Page 74 **Booking ahead**

2 • Για πότε, κύριε Σοφούλη;
• Από τη **Δευτέρα** μέχρι την **Τετάρτη.**
• Για πότε, κυρία Μιχαλοπούλου;
• Από **αύριο** μέχρι το **Σάββατο.**
• Για πότε, κυρία Θωμόγλου;
• Από την **Παρασκευή** μέχρι την **Κυριακή.**
• Για πότε, κύριε Θυμαρά;
• Από **σήμερα** μέχρι **την Τρίτη.**
• **Δυστυχώς το ξενοδοχείο είναι γεμάτο μέχρι αύριο.**
• **ΣΟΦΟΥΛΗΣ**: Monday – Wednesday

• **ΜΙΧΑΛΟΠΟΥΛΟΥ**: tomorrow – Saturday
• **ΘΩΜΟΓΛΟΥ**: Friday – Sunday
• **ΘΥΜΑΡΑΣ**: today – Tuesday
Problem: The hotel is full until tomorrow.

Page 75 **Making requests**

2 • Καλησπέρα. Μπορώ να **έχω το κλειδί μου,** παρακαλώ;
• Ορίστε, **κύριε Βαννά.**
• Ευχαριστώ. Α, και μπορώ να **κάνω ένα τηλέφωνο** από 'δω;
• Βεβαίως!

• Γεια σας! Μπορώ να **κλείσω ένα δωμάτιο;**
• Βεβαίως! Το όνομά σας, παρακαλώ.
• **Δημητρίου.**
• Εντάξει, **κύριε Δημητρίου.** Ένα δίκλινο με μπάνιο για δύο νύχτες.
• Ναι. Μπορώ να **δω το δωμάτιο;**

• Καλημέρα, **κυρία Αγγελοπούλου.** Φεύγετε σήμερα;
• Ναι. Μπορώ να **πληρώσω με Βίζα;**
• Βεβαίως!
Mr Dimitriou wants to book a room and see the room on offer; Mrs Angelopoulou wants to pay by Visa; Mr Vannas wants his key and to make a phone call.

3
α Γειά ας. **Μπορώ να έχω το διαβατήριό μου, παρακαλώ;**
Ορίστε, κυρία Αλεξίου.
β Καλημέρα. **Θέλω να κλείσω ένα μονόκλινο** για αύριο.
γ **Μπορώ να δω το δίκλινο, παρακαλώ;**
Βεβαίως!
δ Μήπως έχετε ψιλά; **Θέλω να πληρώσω το ταξί.**
α (μπ)4.   β (θ)1.   γ (μπ)3.   δ (θ)2.

Page 76 **Put it all together**

I

a **I've booked . . .**
β **Unfortunately**
γ **Can I book . . . ?**
δ **Certainly**
ε **I want to see . . .**

2 *I* δωμάτιο   *2* μονόκλινο
   3 μπάνιο   *4* πόσο   *5* **Τετάρτη**
   6 **πρώτο**

3
a Έχω κλείσει **ένα μονόκλινο με ντους.**
β Θέλω να πληρώσω **με Βίζα**
γ Μπορώ να κάνω **ένα τηλέφωνο;**
δ Μπορώ να έχω **το κλειδί μου;**

Page 77 **Now you're talking!**

I • Καλησπέρα σας. Ορίστε.
   • **Καλησπέρα (σας). Έχω κλείσει ένα δωμάτιο.**
   • Το όνομά σας, παρακαλώ;
   • **(Με λένε) Δήμητρα Κακούλη.**
   • Α ναι . . . ένα μονόκλινο με μπάνιο.
   • **Ναι. Για τρεις νύχτες.**
   • Εντάξει. Το διαβατήριό σας, παρακαλώ.
   • **Ορίστε. Πού είναι το δωμάτιο;**
   • Είναι στο δεύτερο όροφο. Νούμερο 31.

2 • **Μήπως έχετε δωμάτια;**
   • Ναι. Τι δωμάτια θέλετε;
   • **Ένα δίκλινο με μπάνιο και ένα μονόκλινο με ντους.**
   • Για πόσο καιρό;
   • **Για πέντε νύχτες.**
   • Θέλετε στο ισόγειο ή στο δεύτερο όροφο;
   • **Στο δεύτερο όροφο παρακαλώ.**
   • Εντάξει. Το όνομά σας;
   • **Γιάννης Σίμης**

Page 78 **Quiz**

I **για μία νύχτα**   *2* The hotel is full   *3* **από το Σάββατο μέχρι την Τετάρτη**   *4* today - **σήμερα**, tomorrow - **αύριο**   *5* **Τι μπορώ να κάνω;**   *6* **ή**   *7* **Θέλω να κλείσω ένα δίκλινο με ντους**   *8* **Θέλω ένα δωμάτιο στο ισόγειο.**

Goodnight is **Καληνύχτα.**

Unit 9 **Τι ώρα φεύγει;**

Page 80 **Asking about public transport**

2 • Συγνώμη, κάθε πότε έχει λεωφορείο για τη Θεσσαλονίκη;
   • **Κάθε ώρα.**
   • Πού μπορώ να πάρω εισιτήριο;
   • **Στο λεωφορείο.**
I every hour   *2* on the bus

3 • Κάθε πότε έχει αεροπλάνο για την **Κρήτη;**
   • **Κάθε τρεις ώρες.**

   • Συγνώμη, έχει πούλμαν για τη **Λάρνακα** σήμερα;
   • Όχι, δεν έχει σήμερα, έχει **αύριο.**

   • Κάθε πότε έχει φέρρυ-μποτ για τη **Λέσβο;**
   • **Κάθε μέρα** στις **εφτά το πρωί**
I Aeroplane to Crete every three hours
2 Coach to Larnaca tomorrow
3 Ferry to Lesvos every day, 7a.m.

4 Κάθε πότε έχει Δελφίνι για . . .
   . . . την Πάρο; . . . τη Μύκονο; . . . τη Λευκάδα;

Page 81 **Finding out about travel times**

2

a
- Τι ώρα φεύγει το τραίνο για τη Λάρισα;
- Στις **δέκα το πρωί.**
- Και τι ώρα φτάνει;
- Φτάνει στις **δύο το μεσημέρι.**

β
- Τι ώρα φεύγει το τραίνο για την Κόρινθο;
- Φεύγει στις **τρεις και δέκα το μεσημέρι.**
- Τι ώρα φτάνει στην Κόρινθο;
- Φτάνει στις **πέντε και δέκα το απόγευμα.**

γ
- Τι ώρα φεύγει το τραίνο για την Καβάλα;
- Φεύγει στις **εννιά το βράδυ.**
- Και τι ώρα φτάνει;
- Φτάνει στις **εννιά το πρωί.**

Λάρισα	**10.00 π.μ.**	**2.00 μ.μ.**
	4 ώρες	
Κόρινθος	**3.10 μ.μ.**	**5.10 μ.μ.**
	2 ώρες	
Καβάλα	**9.00 μ.μ.**	**9.00 π.μ.**
	12 ώρες	

3

a
- Καλημέρα. Έχει λεωφορείο για τη Γλυφάδα;
- Ναι. Φεύγει σε **είκοσι λεπτά.**

β
- Γεια σας! Τι ώρα φτάνει το τραίνο από τη Λαμία;
- Φτάνει **στις πέντε και μισή το απόγευμα.**

γ
- Έχει τραίνο ή πούλμαν για την Αθήνα σήμερα;
- Ναι. Το τραίνο φεύγει **σε μισή ώρα** και το πούλμαν φεύγει **στις μία η ώρα.**

a **Όχι.** The bus for Glyfada leaves in 20 minutes.
β **Ναι**
γ **Όχι.** The train to Athens leaves in half an hour.

Pages 82 & 83 Buying tickets and checking travel details

2

a
- Θέλω **ένα** εισιτήριο **απλό** για το Ναύπλιο, παρακαλώ.
- Για πότε;
- Για **αύριο το πρωί.**

β
- Θέλουμε **τρία** εισιτήρια για την **Τρίπολη,** με **επιστροφή.**
- Για σήμερα;
- Όχι, για την **Τρίτη.**

γ
- **Ένα** εισιτήριο για το **Βόλο** παρακαλώ.
- Απλό ή με επιστροφή;
- **Απλό** παρακαλώ . . . για **σήμερα το βράδυ.**

δ
Θέλω **ένα εισιτήριο απλό** για τη **Πρέβεζα,** για **σήμερα το απόγευμα.**
Εντάξει.

ε
Θέλουμε **τέσσερα** εισιτήρια για τη **Σπάρτη για αύριο.**
Με επιστροφή;
Ναι, ευχαριστώ.

a Nafplio, 1, single, tomorrow morning
β Tripoli, 3, return, Tuesday
γ Volos, 1, single, this evening
δ Preveza, 1, single, this afternoon
ε Sparta, 4, return, tomorrow

4

a
Συγνώμη, από πού φεύγει το λεωφορείο **για την Αθήνα;**
Από το σταθμό εκεί.

β
Αυτό είναι το λεωφορείο **για τη Θεσσαλονίκη;**
Όχι, το λεωφορείο για τη Θεσσαλονίκη φεύγει **από την πλατεία.**

γ
Το λεωφορείο **για το κέντρο,** από πού φεύγει;
Φεύγει **από το λιμάνι.**

1 Athens – the station. *2* Thessaloniki – the square. *3* The centre – harbour.

5 Πού πάει αυτό το αεροπλάνο /
το τραίνο / το καράβι;

6

1 Το πούλμαν **νούμερο 20 πάει στην
Πάφο**.
2 Το πούλμαν **νούμερο 12 φτάνει
τώρα από την Άγια Νάπα**.
3 Το πούλμαν **νούμερο 1 φεύγει σε
μισή ώρα**.
4 Το πούλμαν **νούμερο 6 από τη
Λεμεσό έχει καθυστέρηση. Φτάνει
σε μισή ώρα**.

*Arriving from Ayia Napa – 12; Going to
Paphos – 20; Delayed arriving in ½ hour – 6;
Leaving in ½ hour – 1.*

Page 84 **Put it all together**

1

α False. Φεύγει στις έξι το πρωί.
β True.
γ True.
δ False. Φτάνει στις δέκα το βράδυ.
ε False. Πάει στη Θεσσαλονίκη.
ζ False. Φτάνει στις τρεις και μισή.

2 • Καλημέρα. Έχει Δελφίνι **για** τη
Σκιάθο αύριο;
• Ναι, **έχει** τέσσερα.
• **Κάθε** πότε φεύγουνε;
• Κάθε δύο **ώρες** από τις οχτώ το
πρωί.
• Πού μπορώ **να** πάρω εισιτήριο;
• Από 'δω. Πόσα **θέλετε**;
• Ένα **εισιτήριο** για τις **δώδεκα** το
μεσημέρι.
• Απλό;
• Όχι, με **επιστροφή**.

Page 85 **Now you're talking!**

1 • **Κάθε πότε έχει φέρρυ-μποτ για
την Αθήνα;**
• Έχει κάθε μέρα το πρωί.
• **Τι ώρα φεύγει;**
• Στις δέκα η ώρα.
• **Πού μπορώ να πάρω εισιτήριο;**
• Στο πρακτορείο.

2 • **Καλημέρα. Θέλω ένα εισιτήριο
απλό για την Αθήνα.**
• Εντάξει. Για πότε είναι;
• **Για σήμερα. Από πού φεύγει;**
• Από το Ακρωτήρι.
• **Αυτό είναι το φέρρυ-μποτ για
την Αθήνα;**
• Ναι. Αυτό είναι.

3 • Τι ώρα φεύγει η πτήση σου;
• **Η πτήση φεύγει στις εφτά το
βράδυ.**
• Και τι ώρα φτάνει στο Λονδίνο;
• **Φτάνει στο Λονδίνο στις οχτώ
και μισή.**
• Το εισιτηριό σου είναι απλό ή με
επιστροφή;
• **Είναι (ένα εισιτήριο) με
επιστροφή.**
• Πόσο κάνει;
• **(Κάνει) εκατόν ενενήντα εννιά
λίρες.**

Page 86 **Quiz**

1 The flight is delayed   2 **ένα εισιτήριο
με επιστροφή**   3 **Φεύγουμε**
4 **σε δύο ώρες**
5 **Πού πάει αυτό το πούλμαν;**
6 Αυτή **η** πτήση – Αυτός **ο** σάκος –
Αυτό **το** τραίνο   7 **κάθε**   8 '**για**'
should be changed to '**από**'
9 **Σήμερα το πρωί.**

Unit 10 **Καλή όρεξη!**

Pages 88 & 89 **Asking what's on the
menu and ordering food and drink**

2 • Καλημέρα. Τι έχετε σήμερα;
• Από ορεκτικά έχουμε **τζατζίκι**,
γίγαντες, και **καλαμαράκια** . . .
Της ώρας έχουμε μόνο **σουβλάκια**
Από κιμάδες έχουμε **μακαρόνια
με κιμά** και πιπεριές γεμιστές.
Και από σαλάτες έχουμε
χωριάτικη μόνο.

Available: Tzatziki, giant beans, squid, kebabs, spaghetti with mince, stuffed peppers and Greek salad.

4 • Τι θα φάτε παρακαλώ;
• Θα πάρουμε μία καλαμαράκια και μία ταραμοσαλάτα παρακαλώ.
• Εντάξει, και μετά;
• Μία **ντομάτες γεμιστές** και μία μακαρόνια με κιμά.
• Θέλετε σαλάτα;
• Ναι. Μία χωριάτικη παρακαλώ . . .
α ναι, και δύο πατάτες τηγανιτές.
*Not on menu; **Stuffed tomatoes**.*

6 • Ορίστε, τι θα πάρετε;
• Εγώ θα πάρω **μία αρνί ψητό**
• Εντάξει. . . και για την κυρία;
• Τι έχετε για χορτοφάγους;
• Έχουμε **γίγαντες και χωριάτικη**.
• Μία γίγαντες παρακαλώ.
• Τι θα πιείτε;
• Έχετε βαρελίσιο κρασί;
• Βεβαίως!
• Θα πάρουμε **ένα κιλό κόκκινο παρακαλώ**.
He orders roast lamb, recommended for Poppy are beans and Greek salad, and they order a litre of red wine from the barrel.

Pages 90 & 91 Expressing likes and dislikes

2 (Δεν) μ'αρέσει η ταραμοσαλάτα
το ψωμί
το τζατζίκι
(Δεν) μ'αρέσουνε οι πιπεριές γεμιστές
οι ντολμάδες
οι πατάτες
τα μακαρόνια με κιμά

3 Τι έχουνε σήμερα; **Η ταραμοσαλάτα δεν μ'αρέσει πολύ. Μ'αρέσει το τζατζίκι. Δεν μ'αρέσουνε καθόλου οι πιπεριές γεμιστές.**
Α . . . μακαρόνια με κιμά μ'αρέσουνε πολύ.
a Likes very much . . . spaghetti with

*mince **7**; β Likes . . . yoghurt and cucumber dip **5**; γ Doesn't like very much . . . taramosalata **3**; δ Doesn't like at all . . . stuffed peppers **1***

5 • Παρακαλώ!
• Ορίστε!
• Μας φέρνετε **ακόμα μισό κιλό ρετσίνα** και **ακόμα μία χωριάτικη σαλάτα** παρακαλώ . . . α, και **ακόμα λίγο τυρί.**
• Ορίστε. Όλα εντάξει;
• Ναι. Μ'αρέσουνε πολύ **οι κεφτέδες σας.**
• Ευχαριστούμε.
Another half litre of retsina, another Greek salad and more cheese. He likes the meatballs.

6
α ακόμα μία κοκακόλα
β ακόμα ένα μπουκάλι κρασί
γ ακόμα λίγο λάδι
δ ακόμα μια φέτα

Page 92 Put it all together

1 α - 4 β - 3 γ - 6 δ - 5 ε - 1
ζ - 7 η - 2

2 **ΟΡΕΚΤΙΚΑ** – τζατζίκι, χταπόδι, καλαμαράκια, ντολμάδες
ΨΗΤΑ – κοτόπουλο, μοσχάρι, χοιρινό, αρνί
ΤΗΣ ΩΡΑΣ – σουβλάκια, μπριζόλες, κεφτέδες, λουκάνικα
ΚΡΑΣΙΑ – ρετσίνα, κόκκινο, ροζέ, άσπρο.

3
α Μ'αρέσ**ουνε** . . . β Σας αρέσ**ει** . . .
γ Δεν μ' αρέσ**ουνε** . . . δ Μ'αρέσ**ει** . . .

4
α ακόμα μία β ακόμα λίγο γ ακόμα ένα δ ακόμα λίγο

Page 93 **Now you're talking!**

- Καλησπέρα σας! Τι θα πιείτε;
- **Μία μπύρα και μισό κιλό άσπρο κρασί παρακαλώ.**
- Εντάξει ... Ορίστε. Τι θα φάτε;
- **Τι έχετε σήμερα;**
- Έχουμε ορεκτικά, μπριζόλες, σουβλάκια, παστίτσιο και γεμιστά.
- **Θα πάρουμε μία καλαμαράκια, μία ταραμοσαλάτα, και ένα τζατζίκι παρακαλώ.**
- Βεβαίως ... και μετά;
- **Σ'αρέσει το παστίτσιο;**
- Όχι πολύ, θα πάρω μία ντομάτες γεμιστές.
- **Δύο ντομάτες γεμιστές, και μία χωριάτικη σαλάτα παρακαλώ.**
- θέλετε πατάτες τηγανιτές;
- **Όχι. Δεν θέλουμε πατάτες τηγανιτές.**
- Ορίστε. Καλή όρεξη!
- **Ευχαριστούμε. Μας φέρνετε ακόμα μία μπύρα παρακαλώ;**
- Θέλετε τίποτ' άλλο;
- **Όχι ευχαριστώ. Το λογαριασμό, παρακαλώ.**

Page 94 **Quiz**

1 **Μ'αρέσουνε** *2* **Μας φέρνετε το λογαριασμό παρακαλώ;** *3* Dishes cooked to order *4* **Δεν** μ'αρέσει η φέτα **καθόλου** *5* **αρνί** (lamb), **μοσχάρι** (veal), **κοτόπουλο** (chicken), **χοιρινό** (pork) *6* **Τι έχετε για χορτοφάγους;** *7* **ακόμα ένα** *8* He wants to know what you want to eat *9* **Καλή όρεξη!** *10* **μία**

Έλεγχος! 3 (Pages 95–98)

1 β **Συγνώμη, πού μπορώ να πάρω ταξί;**

2 • Πού πάτε;
- **Πάω στο Ξενοδοχείο Ηλέκτρα.**
- Εντάξει.

- **Πόσο κάνει;**
- **Δέκα ευρώ και πενήντα λεπτά.**
  Change: € 9,50 *(εννιά ευρώ και πενήντα λεπτά)*

3 • Από πού είσαστε;
- **Είμαι από την Αγγλία.**
- Είσαστε εδώ για δουλειά;
- **Ναι, (είμαι εδώ για δουλειά).**
- Για πόσο καιρό;
- **Για πέντε μέρες.**
- Σας αρέσει η δουλειά σας;
- **Ναι, μ'αρέσει (πολύ). / Όχι, δεν μ'αρέσει (πολύ / καθόλου).**

4 γ **Έχω κλείσει ένα μονόκλινο με ντους από σήμερα μέχρι το Σάββατο.**

5 **Το όνομά σας**, παρακαλώ.
Το διαβατήριό σας, παρακαλώ.
Το δωμάτιό σας είναι νούμερο **εξήντα οχτώ** στο **δεύτερο όροφο**
α *your name*
β *your passport*
γ *Room: 68 – Floor: 2nd*

6 • Πού είναι το πρακτορείο;
- Θα πάτε δεξιά, θα στρίψετε αριστερά στο ταχυδρομείο και μετά θα πάτε ίσια για 100 μέτρα.
  Go right, turn left at the post office and then go straight on for 100 metres.

7
α **Κάθε πότε** έχει λεωφορείο **για** την Καβάλα;
β Τι ώρα **φεύγει** από τη Θεσσαλονίκη;
γ Πόσο **κάνει** ένα εισιτήριο **με επιστροφή**;

8 Το πρώτο λεωφορείο φεύγει από τη Θεσσαλονίκη στις **έξι το πρωί (6.00 π.μ.)** και φτάνει στην Καβάλα στις **εννιά και μισή (9.30)**. Ένα εισιτήριο με επιστροφή κάνει **σαράντα τρία ευρώ και ογδόντα λεπτά.**
Leaves: 6.00 a.m., arrives: 9.30 a.m., price: € 43,80.

- **Τη Δευτέρα είμαστε εδώ στην Καβάλα.**
- **Την Τρίτη έχουμε ραντεβού στην Ξάνθη.**
- **Την Τετάρτη φεύγουμε για τη Δράμα για δύο μέρες.**
- **Την Πέμπτη δουλεύουμε με τον Richard Peters στη Δράμα.**
- **Την Παρασκευή πάμε στη Θάσο για τρεις μέρες.**
- **Την Κυριακή το βράδυ φτάνουμε ξανά στην Καβάλα.**

9 **Ξάνθη** – Tuesday
   Καβάλα – Monday and Sunday evening
   Δράμα – Wednesday and Thursday
   Θάσος – Friday, Saturday and Sunday

10 Mon. (We are) here in Kavala.
    Tues. (We have an) appointment in Xanthi.
    Wed. (We leave for) Drama for 2 days.
    Thur. (We are) working with Richard Peters in Drama.
    Fri. (We go to) Thassos for 3 days.
    Sat. (Thassos)
    Sun. evening – (we arrive back in) Kavala.

11
a **Πού μένεις;**
   Μένω εδώ στην Καβάλα με τη γυναίκα μου.
β **Πώς τη λένε;**
   Τη λένε Νάντια.
γ **Έχεις παιδιά;**
   Ναι, έχω δύο παιδιά.
δ **Πόσο χρονών είναι;**
   Είναι έξι και δέκα χρονών.

12
- Είσαι από την Αγγλία;
- **Ναι. / Όχι, είμαι από την + your country.**
- Πού μένεις εκεί;
- **Μένω στο + your town**
- Πού κοντά είναι;
- **Είναι κοντά στο + your nearest well-known town or city.**
- Σ'αρέσει η Ελλάδα;
- **Ναι, μ'αρέσει πολύ.**
- Τι θα πάρεις;
- **(Θα πάρω) ένα ούζο / μία μπύρα or drink of your choice.**

13
a A fish taverna.
β (one of): fresh fish, seafood, e.g. octopus, squid.
γ **Θαλασσινά.**
δ No. (Closed only on Monday).
ε Greek music.
ζ Wines from the barrel and retsina.
η St. Marina Square, near the sea.

14
a €8,90
β €116
γ €1,75

Grammar

Grammar is simply the term used to describe the patterns of a language. Knowing these patterns will enable you to move away from total reliance on set phrases.

1 **Nouns** (words for people, things, places, concepts, names) are all either masculine (m.) feminine (f.) or neuter (n.).

Singular nouns (one only)	To form the plural (more than one)
a ending in **-ος** (mostly m.)	change to **-οι**
b ending in **-α** or **-η** (mostly f.)	change to **-ες**
c ending in **-ο** or **-ι** (all n.)	change to **-α** or **-ια**
d borrowed words (mostly n.)	no plural form

2 **Articles** (a / an, the) have masculine, feminine and neuter forms.

a / an	the *singular*	the *plural*	the *after* από σε, για, etc.
m. **ένας** δρόμος	**ο** δρόμος	**οι** δρόμοι	**το(ν)** δρόμο
f. **μία** μπύρα	**η** μπύρα	**οι** μπύρες	**τη(ν)** μπύρα
n. **ένα** μήλο	**το** μήλο	**τα** μήλα	**το** μήλο

In Greek 'the' is used with Proper Nouns, e.g. place names:

   ο Βόλος   **το Λονδίνο**   **η Κρήτη**

. . . and people's names, except when you're addressing them directly:

   ο Γιάννης   *but*   **Γεια σου Γιάννη!**

   η Μαρία   *but*   **Γεια σου Μαρία!**

When a masculine or feminine noun comes after **από, σε** and **για**, and begins with **κ, τ, π** or a vowel, then **ν** is added to **το** and **τη**:

από την Κρήτη from Crete   **στον Καναδά** to, in Canada

When asking for masculine objects, e.g. in shops or restaurants, the final **ς** is dropped from both **ένας** and the masculine noun:

	ένας καφές	a / one coffee
but	**ένα καφέ παρακαλώ**	a / one coffee, please

3 **Verbs** (words for doing or being) can be recognized in English because you can put 'to' in front of them: *to live, to have, to work*. This is the 'infinitive' form. In Greek there is no infinitive, so to talk about a verb you use the first person singular, *I live, I have, I work*, **μένω, έχω, δουλεύω**. This is the form that appears in a dictionary.

Regular verbs follow this pattern:

		μένω *to live*	**έχω** *to have*	**δουλεύω** *to work*
I	**εγώ**	**μένω**	**έχω**	**δουλεύω**
you	**εσύ**	**μένεις**	**έχεις**	**δουλεύεις**
he / she	**αυτός / αυτή**	**μένει**	**έχει**	**δουλεύει**
it / this	**αυτό**			
we	**εμείς**	**μένουμε**	**έχουμε**	**δουλεύουμε**
you	**εσείς**	**μένετε**	**έχετε**	**δουλεύετε**
they (m. / f.)	**αυτοί / αυτές**	**μένουν(ε)**	**έχουν(ε)**	**δουλεύουν(ε)**
they (n.)	**αυτά**			

Since the ending of the verb is enough to tell us who is doing something, it's not necessary to use the words *I, you, he / she, we, they* except for emphasis, contrast, or clarification of the *he / she / it* form.

There are two different words for 'you':

εσύ: (singular, informal) a friend, family member or a younger person

εσείς: (plural, formal) someone you don't know well, an older person or more than one person.

Some common verbs don't follow the regular patterns and have to be learnt separately:

		είμαι to be	πάω to go
I	εγώ	είμαι	πάω
you	εσύ	είσαι	πας
he/she/it	αυτός / ή / ό	είναι	πάει
we	εμείς	είμαστε	πάμε
you	εσείς	είσαστε	πάτε
they	αυτοί / ές / ά	είναι	πάνε

There is only one form for the present tense in Greek and it expresses the two forms of the present tense in English: 'I work' and 'I'm working'.

4 Questions and negative statements

To ask a question:
1) simply change the intonation of your voice to a rising tone –
('closed' questions), or
2) start your question with one of these words – ('open' questions):

Τι;	What?	**Πού;**	Where?
Πότε;	When?	**Πώς;**	How?
Πόσο;	How much?	**Πόσα;**	How many?

To make a statement negative the word **δεν** is placed before the verb,

Δεν είμαι από την Ελλάδα.   I'm not from Greece.
Ο Κώστας δεν είναι εδώ.   Costas isn't here.

5 Possession

To express possession or 'belonging' the word 'the' precedes the noun and the appropriate possessive word follows the noun.

το παιδί **μου**	my child
το παιδί **σου**	your child (singular / informal)
το παιδί **του**	his child
το παιδί **της**	her child
(**το** παιδί **του**)	(its child)
το παιδί **μας**	our child
το παιδί **σας**	your child (plural / formal)
το παιδί **τους**	their child
η φίλη **μου** etc.	my female friend etc.
ο άντρας **μου** etc.	my husband etc.

6 Μ'αρέσει / Μ'αρέσουνε

Μ' is an abbreviation of **μου** (meaning 'to me'). The Greek for 'I like . . .' literally means 'To me is / are pleasing . . .'

Μ'αρέσει το κρασί.	I like wine.
(To me is pleasing the wine.)	
Μ'αρέσουνε τα σουβλάκια.	I like kebabs.
(To me are pleasing the kebabs.)	

To talk about what others like or don't like, you use the following words before **αρέσει** and **αρέσουνε**:

σου / σ'	'to you' (singular / informal)
του	'to him'
της	'to her'
μας	'to us'
σας	'to you' (plural / formal)
τους	'to them'

To express dislike, the word **δεν** is placed before **μου**, **σου**, etc.

Δεν μου / μ'αρέσει το ψάρι.	I don't like fish.
Δεν του αρέσει η ρετσίνα.	He doesn't like retsina.
Δεν μας αρέσουνε οι ελιές.	We don't like olives.

Greek–English glossary

This glossary contains only those words and phrases and their meanings that occur in this book.

A

η Αγγλία *England*
    αγγλικό *English*
ο Άγγλος *Englishman*
η Αγγλίδα *Englishwoman*
το αγγούρι *cucumber*
το αγόρι *boy*
το αεροπλάνο *aeroplane*
η Αθήνα *Athens*
    ακόμα ένα / μία *another (one)*
    αλλά *but*
    άλλο *other*
ο Αμερικανός *American man*
η Αμερικανίδα *American woman*
η Αμερική *America*
η αν. (αναχώρηση) *departure*
    ανοίγω *to open (I open)*
το αντηλιακό *suntan lotion*
    αντίο *goodbye*
ο άντρας *man, husband*
    απέναντι από *opposite*
    απλό *simple, single*
    από *from*
    από 'δώ *from here*
το απόγευμα *afternoon, early evening*
    αρέσω *to please:*
    μ'αρέσει / μ'αρέσουνε *I like it / them*
    αριστερά *(on the) left*
το αρνί *lamb*
το ΑΡΤΟΠΩΛΕΙΟΝ *baker's*
το ασανσέρ *lift*
η ασπιρίνη *aspirin*

    άσπρο *white*
    αύριο *tomorrow*
η Αυστραλία *Australia*
ο Αυστραλός *Australian man*
η Αυστραλέζα *Australian woman*
    αυτά! *that's all!*
    αυτό / αυτά *this / these (n.)*
    αυτοί *these (m. pl.), these people*
    αυτός / αυτή *he, she*
η αφ. (άφιξη) *arrival*

B

    βαρελίσιο *(from the) barrel*
    βεβαίως! *Certainly! (Sure!)*
το Βερολίνο *Berlin*
το βιβλίο *book*
η βότκα *vodka*
το βούτυρο *butter*
το βράδυ *evening*

Γ

το γάλα *milk*
    γεια σας, γεια σου *hello (formal / informal)*
    γεμάτο *full*
    γεμιστά *stuffed vegetables*
    για *for*
    για μένα *for me*
το γιαούρτι *yoghurt*
οι γίγαντες *butter beans*
το γκαράζ *garage*
το γκολφ *golf*
    γλυκό *sweet*
το γραμματόσημο *stamp*

το γραφείο *office*
η γυναίκα *woman, wife*

Δ

    δέκα ten
το Δελφίνι *the 'Flying Dolphin' hydrofoil*
οι Δελφοί *Delphi*
    δεν *(used with verbs) not*
    – δεν κατάλαβα *I didn't understand*
    δεξιά *(on the) right*
η Δευτέρα *Monday*
    δεύτερο *second*
το διαβατήριο *passport*
οι διακοπές *holidays*
το διαμέρισμα *flat, apartment*
το δίκλινο *double room*
    δίπλα σε *next to*
ο δρόμος *road*
η διψομανία *dipsomania (thirst)*
το Δουβλίνο *Dublin*
η δουλειά *work*
    δουλεύω *to work, (I work)*
    δύο *two*
    δυστυχώς *unfortunately*
    δω (βλέπω), *(to see) –*
    θέλω να δω *I want to see*
τα Δωδεκάνησα *the Dodecanese*
το δωμάτιο *room*
το δώρο *present, gift*

E

	εγώ *I*
το	Εδιμβούργο *Edinburgh*
	εδώ *here*
η	εικόνα *picture, icon*
	είμαι *I am*
το	εισιτήριο *ticket*
	εκατό(ν) *a, one hundred*
	εκεί *there*
η	εκκλησία *church*
ο	έλεγχος *check,* *checkpoint*
η	ελιά *olive*
η	Ελλάδα *Greece*
ο	Έλληνας *Greek man*
η	Ελληνίδα *Greek woman*
τα	ελληνικά *Greek (language)* – στα ελληνικά *in Greek* ελληνικό *Greek (adj.)*
	ένα / μία *a, one*
	εννιά *nine*
	ΕΝΟΙΚΙΑΖΟΝΤΑΙ *for hire, for rent*
	εντάξει *all right, OK*
η	επιστροφή *return* – με επιστροφή *(ticket) with return*
	εσείς / εσύ *you (formal / informal)*
το	εστιατόριο *restaurant*
	έτσι κ'έτσι *so-so*
το	ευρώ *euro*
	ευχαριστώ *(I) thank you* – ευχαριστούμε *(we) thank you*
η	εφημερίδα *newspaper*
	έχει *there is, there are*
	έχω *to have (I have)*

Z

| το | ζαμπόν *ham* |

H

| | ή *or* |
| η | *the (f.)* |

Θ

| | θα πάρω (παίρνω) *I'll take (to take)* |
| | θα πάτε (πάω) *you'll go* |

	(to go)
	θα στρίψετε (στρίβω) *you'll turn (to turn)*
	θα πιείτε (πίνω) *you will drink (I drink)* – Τι θα πιείτε; *What will you drink?*
	θα φάτε (τρώω) *you will eat (I eat)* – Τι θα φάτε; *What will you eat?*
η	θάλασσα *sea*
τα	θαλασσινά *seafood*
το	θέατρο *theatre*
	θέλω *to want (I want)*

I

η	Ιρλανδία *Ireland*
ο/η	Ιρλανδός / Ιρλανδέζα *Irish man / Irish woman*
	ίσια *straight on*
το	ΙΧΘΥΟΠΩΛΕΙΟΝ *fishmonger's*

K

	κάθε *every*
	καθόλου *(not) at all*
η	καθυστέρηση *delay*
	και *and*
ο	καιρός *time*
	καλά *well*
τα	καλαμαράκια *squid*
	καλημέρα *good morning*
	καληνύχτα *good night*
	καλησπέρα *good afternoon, evening*
το	κάμπινγκ *campsite*
το	κανταΐφι *sweet Greek pastry*
	κάνω *to do / make (I make)*
	Τι κάνετε; *How are you?*
	Πόσο κάνει; *How much is it?*
το	καπέλο *hat*
το	καπουτσίνο *cappuccino*
το	καράβι *boat / ship*
η	κάρτα *card, postcard*
το	καρπούζι *watermelon*
	κατάλαβα (καταλαβαίνω)

	I understood (to understand / I understand)
το	καφενείο *coffee house*
η	καφετερία *cafeteria*
ο	καφές *coffee*
το	κέντρο *centre*
η	Κέρκυρα *Corfu*
οι	κεφτέδες *meatballs*
το	κιλό *kilo*
οι	ΚΙΜΑΔΕΣ *minced meat dishes*
το	κλειδί *key*
	κλείνω *to close, to book:* έχω κλείσει *I have booked*
η	κλινική *clinic*
η	κοκακόλα *coca cola*
	κόκκινο *red*
το	κολλέγιο *college*
το	κομπολόϊ *(set of) worry beads*
	κοντά *near, nearby* – κοντά σε *near to*
το	κορίτσι *girl*
το	κοτόπουλο *chicken*
το	κρασί *wine*
η	Κρήτη *Crete*
ο	Κύπριος *Cypriot man*
η	Κύπρια *Cypriot woman*
η	Κύπρος *Cyprus*
η	κυρία *lady*
	Κυρία *Mrs*
η	Κυριακή *Sunday*
ο	κύριος *gentleman*
	Κύριος *Mr*
	'Γεια σας, Κύριε . . .' *'Hello, Mr . . .'*

Λ

το	λάδι *oil*
η	Λεμεσός *Limassol*
η	λεμονάδα *lemonade*
το	λεμόνι *lemon*
το	λεπτό *minute / euro cent*
	λέτε (λέω) *you say (to say)* – το λέτε ξανά; *Can you say it again?*
η	Λευκάδα *Lefkada, Lefkas*
η	Λευκωσία *Nicosia*
το	λεωφορείο *bus*

λίγο a little
το   λιμάνι harbour
η   λίρα pound (currency)
ο   λογαριασμός bill
το   Λονδίνο London
το   λουκάνικο sausage

Μ

μ.μ. p.m.
το   μαγαζί shop
η   Μαδρίτη Madrid
τα   μακαρόνια με κιμά
      spaghetti with mince
      μακριά far (away)
      μακριά από far from
η   μαρμελάδα jam
      με with
      με me
      με λένε I'm called
      (lit: they call me)
η   Μελβούρνη Melbourne
οι   μελιτζάνες τηγανιτές
      fried aubergines
      μένω to live (I live)
η   μέρα day
το   μεσημέρι midday
      period
      μετά then, after
το   Μεταξά Metaxa (Greek
      brandy)
      μέτριο medium
το   μέτρο metre
      μέχρι until
      μηδέν zero
το   μήλο apple
      μήπως (έχετε;) by any
      chance (do you have?)
      μισή, μισό half
το   μοναστήρι monastery
      μόνο only
το   μονόκλινο single room
το   μοσχάρι veal
      μου / μας my / our
ο   μουσακάς moussaka
το   μουσείο museum
η   μουσική music
ο   μπακλαβάς sweet Greek
      pastry
το   μπαλκόνι balcony
το   μπάνιο bathroom

το   μπαρ bar
το   μπισκότο biscuit
      μπορώ (να) to be able (to)
      I can
το   μπουκάλι bottle
η   μπουτίκ boutique
το   μπρέκφαστ breakfast
      μπρέκφαστ κοντινεντάλ
      continental breakfast
η   μπριζόλα (meat) chop,
      cutlet
η   μπύρα beer

Ν

      ναι yes
η   Νέα Υόρκη New York
το   νερό water
το   Νεσκαφέ instant coffee
το   νοσοκομείο hospital
το   νούμερο number
η   ντισκοτέκ disco
οι   ντολμάδες stuffed vine
      leaves
η   ντομάτα tomato
το   ντους shower
η   νύχτα night

Ξ

      ξανά again
το   ξενοδοχείο hotel

Ο

      ο, η, το the (m., f., n.)
      sing.
      οι, οι, τα the (m., f., n.)
      plural
η   οικογένεια family
      όλο / όλα all, everything
      (s. / pl.)
η   ομελέτα omelette
η   ομπρέλλα umbrella
το   όνομα name
η   Οξφόρδη Oxford
το   ΟΠΩΡΟΠΑΝΤΟΠΩΛΕΙΟΝ
      general and greengrocer's
      store
το   ΟΠΩΡΟΠΩΛΕΙΟΝ
      greengrocer's
τα   ΟΡΕΚΤΙΚΑ
      appetisers, starters

η   όρεξη appetite – καλή
      όρεξη! Enjoy your meal!
      ορίστε 'Here you are' /
      'Yes?' / 'Yes, please?'
ο   όροφος floor, storey
ο   Ο.Τ.Ε. Greek
      Telecommunications
      Organization
η   Ουαλία Wales
ο   Ουάλος Welshman
η   Ουαλή Welsh woman
το   ούζο ouzo
το   ουίσκι whisky
      όχι no
      οχτώ eight

Π

      π.μ. a.m.
ο   πάγος ice
το   παγωτό ice cream
το   παιδί child,
ο   Παναθηναϊκός
      Panathinaikos, Athenian
      football team
το   ΠΑΝΤΟΠΩΛΕΙΟΝ
      general grocer's
      παρά but for – (μία)
      παρά δέκα ten to (one)
      παρακαλώ please, you're
      welcome
η   παραλία seafront, beach,
      promenade
η   Παρασκευή Friday
το   Παρίσι Paris
η   πάστα cake, gateau
το   παστίτσιο macaroni pie
οι   πατάτες τηγανιτές
      fried potatoes, chips
      πάω to go (I go)
η   Πελοπόννησος the
      Peloponnese
η   Πέμπτη Thursday
      πέντε five
το   περίπτερο kiosk
το   πιάτο plate, dish
      πιο αργά more slowly
οι   πιπεριές γεμιστές
      stuffed peppers
η   πίτσα (ατομική)
      (individual) pizza

η	πλατεία square
	πληρώσω (πληρώνω),
	(to pay / I pay) – θέλω να
	πληρώσω I want to pay
	πολύ very (much)
το	πορτοκάλι orange
	πόσα; how many?
	πόσο / πόση; how
	much?
	πόσο χρονών; how
	old?
	πότε; when?
το	ποτό drink
	πού where? – από πού;
	where from?
το	πούλμαν coach
το	πρακτορείο (ticket)
	agency
το	πρωί morning
	πρώτο first
η	πτήση flight
	πώς; how?

Ρ

το	ραντεβού appointment,
	rendezvous
η	ρετσίνα retsina
	ροζέ rosé

Σ

το	Σάββατο Saturday
το	σαγανάκι fried cheese
οι	σαγιονάρες flip-flops
ο	σάκος bag, holdall
οι	ΣΑΛΑΤΕΣ salads
το	σάντουϊτς sandwich
	σε to, in: στο(ν) /
	στη(ν) / στο to, in the
	(m. / f. / n.)
	σήμερα today
	σκέτο plain, with nothing
	added
η	Σκωτία Scotland
ο	Σκωτσέζος Scottish
	man
η	Σκωτσέζα Scottish
	woman
το	σνακμπάρ snack bar
η	σόδα soda water
η	σοκολάτα (bar of)

	chocolate – σοκολάτα
	ζεστή hot chocolate
	σου / σας your (formal /
	informal)
τα	σουβλάκια kebabs
το	σουπερμάρκετ
	supermarket
οι	σπεσιαλιτέ specialities
το	Σπράϊτ Sprite
ο	σταθμός station
το	σταφύλι grape
	συγνώμη sorry,
	excuse me
	συγχαρητήρια!
	congratulations!
το	σχολείο school

Τ

	τα the (neuter plural)
η	ταβέρνα taverna
το	τάβλι backgammon
το	ταξί taxi
το	ταξίδι journey – καλό
	ταξίδι! Have a good
	journey!
ο	ταξιτζής taxi driver
η	ταραμοσαλάτα cod roe
	dip, taramosalata
η	ταράτσα terrace
το	ταχυδρομείο post office
	τέσσερα / τέσσερις
	four
η	Τετάρτη Wednesday
το	τέταρτο quarter (of an
	hour) – (μία) και
	τέταρτο quarter past
	(one) – ένα τέταρτο
	(κιλό) a quarter (of a
	kilo)
το	τζατζίκι yoghurt and
	cucumber dip
το	τζιν gin
η	τηλεκάρτα telephone
	card
το	τηλέφωνο telephone
η	Τήνος Tinos, Greek island
	ΤΗΣ ΩΡΑΣ (dishes)
	cooked to order
	τι; what?
η	τιμή price

το	ΤΙΜΟΛΟΓΙΟΝ Price List
	τίποτα anything, nothing
	τίποτ' άλλο; anything
	else?
	το the (n.)
το	τόνικ tonic water
το	τοστ toasted sandwich
	του / της his / her
η	τουαλέτα toilet
το	τουριστικό γραφείο
	tourist office
το	τραίνο train
η	τράπεζα bank
η	τρία / τρεις three
η	Τρίτη Tuesday
το	τσάϊ tea
το	τσιγάρο cigarette
το	τυρί cheese
η	τυρόπιττα cheese pie
	τώρα now

Υ

η	υγεία health – Στην
	υγεία σας / σου / μας!
	Cheers!
	υπάρχει there is

Φ

το	φαρμακείο chemist's
το	ΦΑΣΤ ΦΟΥΝΤ fast
	food (bar)
	φέρνω to bring: (I bring)
	Μας φέρνετε . . . ;
	Can you bring us . . . ?
το	φέρρυ-μποτ ferry
η	φέτα feta cheese
	φεύγω to leave, depart
	(I leave, depart)
το	φιλμ film (for camera)
ο	φίλος male friend
η	φίλη female friend
ο	φούρνος baker's
	φρέσκο fresh
το	φρούτο (piece of) fruit:
	τα φρούτα pieces of
	fruit
	φτάνω to arrive
	(I arrive)

Χ

χαίρω πολύ *pleased to meet you*

το   χοιρινό *pork*

το   χόμπυ *hobby*

ο/η χορτοφάγος *vegetarian (m. / f.)*

το   χταπόδι *octopus*

ο   χυμός *fresh juice*

η   χωριάτικη σαλάτα *Greek salad*

χωρίς *without*

Ψ

το   ψάρι *fish*

η   ψαροταβέρνα *fish taverna*

τα   ΨΗΤΑ *roast meats*

τα   ψιλά *(small) change*

το   ψωμί *bread*

Ω

η   ώρα *hour, time*

Now you're talking

BBC Languages publish a range of resources enabling you to continue improving your Greek.

Greek Language & People

Greek Language & People is the ideal next step to *Talk Greek*. As well as teaching the skills necessary to communicate in and understand basic Greek, it provides an accessible introduction to the written language, and enables you to read Greek with ease. Language practice is mixed with fascinating insights into contemporary Greece and traditional Greek customs.

■ **256pp course book** ■ **2 x audio CDs**

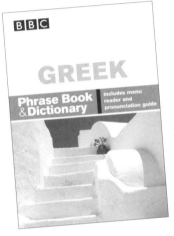

Greek Phrase Book & Dictionary

Practical, concise and easy to use, the *Greek Phrase Book & Dictionary* is the ideal travelling companion. Packed with all the language you'll need in any travel or holiday situation, it will help you get the most out of your trip to Greece.

Get By in Greek

This pocket-sized book is a beautifully illustrated, all-in-one language and travel guide. Find out about all aspects of travel in Greece, from the bare necessities of 'yes' and 'no' to where to eat and sleep, including how to get there, shopping and other entertainment. A travel pack containing book and audio cassette is also available.